CHARLES DICKENS'S SECRET LOVECHILD

Charles Dickens's Secret Lovechild

An Untarnished Portrait of
Ellen Ternan

Brian Ruck

AN IMPRINT OF PEN & SWORD BOOKS LTD.
YORKSHIRE – PHILADELPHIA

First published in Great Britain in 2025 by
Pen & Sword History
An imprint of
Pen & Sword Books Ltd
Yorkshire - Philadelphia

Copyright © Brian Ruck, 2025

ISBN 978 1 03612 932 3

The right of Brian Ruck to be identified as the Author of this work has been asserted by him in accordance with the Copyright, Designs and Patents Act 1988.

A CIP catalogue record for this book is available from the British Library.

All rights reserved. No part of this book may be reproduced, transmitted, downloaded, decompiled or reverse engineered in any form or by any means, electronic or mechanical including photocopying, recording or by any information storage and retrieval system, without permission from the Publisher in writing. No part of this book may be used or reproduced in any manner for the purpose of training artificial intelligence technologies or systems.

Typeset in INDIA by IMPEC eSolutions
Printed and bound in England by CPI (UK) Ltd.

The Publisher's authorised representative in the EU for product safety is Authorised Rep Compliance Ltd., Ground Floor, 71 Lower Baggot Street, Dublin D02 P593, Ireland.
www.arccompliance.com

For a complete list of Pen & Sword titles please contact

PEN & SWORD BOOKS LIMITED
47 Church Street, Barnsley, South Yorkshire, S70 2AS, England
E-mail: enquiries@pen-and-sword.co.uk
Website: www.pen-and-sword.co.uk

or

PEN AND SWORD BOOKS
1950 Lawrence Rd, Havertown, PA 19083, USA
E-mail: uspen-and-sword@casematepublishers.com
Website: www.penandswordbooks.com

This book is dedicated to my very good friend and mentor in all things Dickensian, Dr Alan Dilnot. Were it not for Alan, this work would never have been started, let alone completed.

Also to Ann, my very dear wife of 60 years who has for the past decade uncomplainingly tolerated the presence of this 'other woman' in our lives!

Contents

Prologue		viii
Introduction		ix
Chapter One	A Very Brief Biography of Charles Dickens, Up to 1857	1
Chapter Two	Ellen Grows Up	19
Chapter Three	Growing Apart	41
Chapter Four	Plans for Making Reparation	52
Chapter Five	Making Reparation, Plan B	67
Chapter Six	The Last Four Novels	76
Chapter Seven	Ellen 1870–1913	84
Chapter Eight	The Search for Evidence is On!	94
Chapter Nine	Dismantling the Wright/Storey Story	110
Chapter Ten	Other Odds and Sods of 'Evidence'	128
Epilogue and Post Script		144
Acknowledgements		147
Appendix: Dramatis Personae		150
References		176
Index		179

Prologue

Seeking Ellen
In Search of an Untarnished Portrait

Dickens was dead. There is no doubt whatever about that. The register of his burial was signed by the clergyman, the clerk, the undertaker, and the chief mourner. Dickens was as dead as a door-nail. The burial, at his new address, Poets Corner, Westminster Abbey, was witnessed by fourteen mourners, but only thirteen had been named in the 'official' list. The one doubt, then, surrounding this whole event was who was the mysterious fourteenth mourner?

The most likely suspect appears to be one Miss Ellen Lawless Ternan, but if that is the case, one might ask who was she? What was her relationship to Charles Dickens? And why was she there at an apparently private burial service, but not on the list? This small volume is a personal account of my search for an untarnished portrait of Ellen.

Introduction

A bit about myself, my work and my involvement with Dickens

Everybody said so. Far be it from me to assert that what everybody says must be true. Everybody is, often, as likely to be wrong as right. In the general experience, everybody has been wrong so often, and it has taken, in most instances, such a weary while to find out how wrong, that the authority is proved to be fallible. (Charles Dickens; *The Haunted Man*)

******

The truth of something is not determined by the number and status of those who *believe* it to be true. Under that system, all you have is a hypothesis, crushed by that weight until it is fossilised and set in stone, and then *accepted* as a fact which everyone *believes*. But it still remains just a hypothesis. In order to convert it into a fact, there must be irrefutable, incontrovertible evidence. Mere circumstantial evidence, and repeated hearsay and gossip, will not suffice. There was a time when everybody said that the sun revolved around the earth. It was so obviously true. The sun rose in the morning, moved overhead across the sky, and set in the evening every day. Of course it was going round the earth, and no one thought of looking for any other explanation. That was until Copernicus provided an alternative, that being, the sun stayed in one place, and it was the earth rotating on its axis that gave the impression of the sun rising and setting. And he didn't just say it, he actually demonstrated it mathematically and we now know it to be a proven fact.

But in the case of Charles Dickens and Ellen Ternan, I find nearly everyone saying that Dickens took the young Ellen Ternan as his mistress, and they had a child together. In fact, as Angus Wilson said,[1] very little is *known* about that relationship, and it is amazing how so much has been written about that very little. But the vast majority of what has been written only repeats the same narrative, all still based solely on opinion and belief, just like those who believed the sun went round the earth. Every snippet of information that struggled into the light has been interpreted in such a way as to support what I call the Wright/Storey narrative. Now I am no Copernicus, but I firmly believe that it would be very worthwhile, even essential, to at least look at the possibility that there might be some other explanation for what we can see.

Before I go any further I will say here and now that not only am I no Copernicus, I am by no means a recognised literary expert or Dickens scholar. My life to date (80+ years) has been spent in science, more specifically molecular biology and virology. Initially, I worked in polio vaccine testing laboratories before transferring into biochemical research. The work there was characterising the RNA-dependent RNA polymerase enzyme of influenza virus, some of the very early steps along the sixty-year route toward the development of modern antiviral medicines and the mRNA vaccines which have helped the world through the recent Covid pandemic. I also developed and patented a rapid antigen test (now commonly known as RATs) for hepatitis B. In 1971 I migrated to Australia and joined the University of Melbourne Department of Microbiology, where I became part of the team comprising another scientist at the university and clinicians at the Royal Children's Hospital working on infantile gastroenteritis. With their access to clinical material, and our electron microscope, we were able to discover the cause of the disease, a virus now known as Rotavirus, and for which there are now vaccines available. Shortly after publishing those findings, I decided on a career change and relocated to Monash University, Melbourne. For the last part of my working life I was Manager of the Faculty of Medicine at that university.

I am mentioning all this not to big-note myself, but to say that throughout that life of research we were constantly asking the question Copernicus asked himself: 'Are there any other possible explanations for what we are observing?'

That question was always there, and had to be answered before we could be certain that what we were doing, saying, and writing was actually the truth, and not just our hypotheses. Even in my more managerial role toward the end of my university career, though no longer conducting research myself, I was still very closely associated with the research conducted at the university and within the research institutes with which it was affiliated. I retained my interest in research, and on many occasions heard that same question asked.

Shortly after retiring I returned to classic literature, an area I had abandoned at school in favour of concentrating on science. I was persuaded to attend the Melbourne Branch of the Charles Dickens Fellowship and have been an active member ever since, even serving as President.

Not having read a Dickens novel for many years, despite owning an almost complete set, I thought that as a member of the Fellowship, I should start reading. I read all I had in my own collection, and also started reading books *about* Charles Dickens, which I found to outnumber those *by* Dickens by many orders of magnitude. Quite by chance, the first biography I took from the shelves of Monash University library was one by Michael Harrison.[2] For the first few pages it was quite interesting, Harrison describing a stroll through Rochester looking at buildings and places that Dickens himself would have known. Interesting, because I had been to Rochester several times, but not at all in the last fifty years or so. But then I read, without any previous introduction, a reference to one Ellen Ternan, with the epithet of her being Dickens's little gold-digging mistress. She is mentioned several times through the book, and each time described by that epithet, or a variety of it. He also describes Ellen as an inveterate self-improver, a congenital climber and an Autolycus. He went on further, to claim that she had a grasping nature because she later married a clergyman who became the Head Master of a school in a decayed seaside town.

It mattered not one jot to me whether Dickens had a mistress or not. After all, for many celebrities today, having a lover or a mistress is almost a badge of honour. But what I had difficulty with were the constant vitriolic attacks by Harrison on the character of Ellen Ternan and her mother. And this difficulty was in no way alleviated as I sought the sources of Harrison's opinions. His book mentioned names such as Thomas Wright and Gladys Storey, whose books I later borrowed and read. Harrison failed to provide any reasonable evidence to support his opinions of Ellen's character, other than the eight words spoken by Bella Wilfer in *Our Mutual Friend*: 'I hate being poor, Pa. I want money', and the assumption that Bella Wilfer is a reflection of Ellen Ternan based on the extremely simplistic similarity between the names. I later found that this had been first suggested by Thomas Wright[3] in his biography of Dickens, where he states that any interpretation of the last four novels not taking Ellen into account will be awry.

As I was reading Harrison's book, I very quickly came to the conclusion that what I was reading about Ellen Ternan was nothing more than his closed-mind opinion of her, and in terms of discovering anything about the relationship between Dickens and Ellen, the rest of his book had nothing useful to say. The 'decayed seaside town' to which Harrison referred is Margate, on the very eastern-most point of the Kent coast. I had lived in Margate for several years, and while it is true that Margate had fallen a little in popularity as a holiday destination as new rail links were established with other south-coast towns ahead of those with Margate, by the mid-1870s, it was definitely on the way up again. The Theatre Royal, built in 1787, was magnificently remodelled in 1874, new hotels and roads were being established, and a new skating rink constructed in 1875. So at the time that Ellen and her husband moved there, it was beginning to thrive again. Harrison's description of Margate being 'decayed' and his rather pejorative comment about Ellen's marriage are nothing more than the bias he had against her.

I was determined to discover more about the close relationship that clearly existed between Charles Dickens the author, and Ellen Ternan the actress. Was it carnal, as described in the Wright/Storey narrative and believed by most people? Was it purely platonic as a few, but very small minority, of people believe? Or could it have been a relationship that – though no one had taken a hint from Angus Wilson seriously – was indeed filial?

In this little book I shall review what is actually known as fact, what is believed, and what evidence exists. I shall go on to test the veracity of the evidence, and attempt to answer that perennial question that was always coming to my mind through more than thirty years of scientific research – 'Are there any other explanations that could account for what we are observing?' The explanation currently holding centre stage is, of course, that following their acting together in the Wilkie Collins play *The Frozen Deep* at Manchester in 1857, the then 45-year-old Dickens seduced the then 18-year-old actress, who remained as his mistress until his death in June 1870 and, at some indeterminate stage along the way, gave birth to his child.

I returned Harrison's book to the library and looked for those written by Thomas Wright and by Gladys Storey.[4] But despite there being some 40 metres of shelving holding books about Dickens, these authors were not among them. Clearly, they had not been great sellers, perhaps in part because they were published just before the start of the Second World War, and perhaps in part because they were of very limited interest to the general book-buying population. Whatever the reason, they were rather like the proverbial hen's teeth, and very difficult to find. However, the privileges that came with my honorary appointment included that of making interlibrary loan requests, which I promptly lodged. In the meantime, while waiting for Wright and Storey to appear, I started reading John Forster's *Life of Dickens*,[5] assuming that I would find some description of Ellen that I could compare with Harrison's, and find out a little more about her. Being new to Forster's biography of Dickens, and given that she appeared to be a very important figure in his life, I was surprised to find that the only mention of Ellen in this biography was to be found in the appendix at the back of the book, where Forster had included the Last Will and Testament of Charles Dickens, containing the clause:

> I, Charles Dickens, of Gadshill Place, Higham in the county of Kent, hereby revoke all my former Wills and Codicils and declare this to be my last Will and Testament. I give the sum of £1000 free of legacy duty to Miss Ellen Lawless Ternan, late of Houghton Place, Ampthill Square, in the county of Middlesex.

So, given Harrison's very uncomplimentary descriptions of Ellen on the one hand, and Forster's leaving her out completely on the other, I felt I still had rather a long road ahead if I was ever to get somewhere near the real Ellen Ternan. Forster's *Life of Charles Dickens* added nothing to my store of information about Ellen, but it was not long before the library contacted me with the news that the books by Thomas Wright and Gladys Storey had been found and were available for me to collect.

What I found in Wright's *Life of Dickens* (1935) was very disappointing. Basically, all he said was that he and his friends had long been aware that Ellen Ternan had been Dickens's mistress, but they had no proof; and the sentence already mentioned above, that any interpretation of the last four novels not taking Ellen into consideration would be awry. The names of the main female characters in three of these novels are, of course, Estella, Bella, and Helena, but I am not convinced that the similarity of the names could be interpreted as evidence of a sexual relationship. Similarly, such information as he supplied about various addresses that he discovered Ellen to have lived at, provided nothing substantial about her relationship with Dickens.

And then in his autobiography,[6] he claimed to have been told by the Reverend William Benham, quondam vicar of St John's Church, Margate, that Ellen had been Dickens's mistress. Ellen had moved to Margate in 1877 after her marriage to Thomas Wharton Robinson in 1876, and according to Wright, had 'disburdened her soul to Benham, and had told him the whole story' (of how she had been Dickens's mistress). One of the major weaknesses of Wright's version of events is that William Benham had died on 30 July 1910, some twenty-five years prior to Wright's publication, and hence no one was able to speak with Benham to verify Wright's claim. Ellen herself did not die until 1914 and her two children were also still very much alive. Since Wright claimed to have been given the information earlier than 1910, is it likely that Benham would have broken the confidence of one of his older parishioners while she and her children were still alive? I would hope not. If he had, he was a pretty shabby sort of vicar. It also seemed strange that

Wright first discloses his opinion of Ellen Ternan in his 1935 biography of Dickens, but leaves the source of his information out of that book only to include it in his autobiography a year later. If he had been told anything by Benham that would have occurred at least twenty-five years prior to Wright publishing the biography, and it appears that Wright may have deliberately delayed making his information public until after Ellen's death, and after the death of the last of Dickens's children. However, he did publish his opinion while Ellen's two children were still alive, which was a little insensitive.

At the time of Wright's publication, there was no person living who could confirm or refute his claims, and Wright himself died just prior to the publication of his autobiography, so even he could not be challenged. Wright was only about 8 years old when Dickens died, and it would be most unlikely that he would have had any lived experience of, and been privy to, the sex life of Dickens and Ellen. Thus, he could only have heard about it from rumours picked up later in his life, from his interpretation of Dickens's 'Violated Letter' and 'Personal Statement', (two letters that Dickens wrote in the heat of the separation from Catherine, which received greater publicity than perhaps he intended) which were in the public domain (see later), and perhaps some other unknown sources. Thus, insofar as Wright's contribution is concerned, all that remains to this day is nothing more than second-, third-, or even more-hand completely unsubstantiated hearsay, and certainly cannot be considered as irrefutable evidence.

Much the same can be said of the book *Dickens and Daughter* by Gladys Storey, published in 1939. This book is mostly a stream of trivia about the people who visited the aging Kate

Perugini (Katey Dickens), the youngest surviving daughter of Dickens, during her last years. According to Storey, she had been asked by Katey to write a book telling the story of Dickens and his relationship with her. It is based not on interviews, but on conversations that occurred between whoever was present for afternoon tea at Katey's apartment late in her life. Katey, by this time ailing, was pretty much confined to one chair in her apartment, but nonetheless had many visitors, prominent among them being Gladys Storey and her mother, with one, the other, or generally both, there on most occasions. Gladys kept notes of these afternoon teas, (now available and collectively referred to as 'The Storey Papers'), and as mentioned above, resulted in her book being a rather tiresome description of the dresses and hairstyles of the visitors, and the three-cornered sandwiches and stale cakes served up at tea. Much of it is in Storey's voice, with the occasional quotes from Katey in her voice, indicated by inverted commas, or by the words 'Mrs Perugini said....' or 'Mrs Perugini told the author...'. In the whole book, there is but one sentence referring to Ellen bearing a child fathered by Dickens:

> More tragic and far reaching in its effects was the association of Charles Dickens and Ellen Ternan and their resultant son (who died in infancy), than that of Nelson and Lady Hamilton and their daughter.

And that is all; no mention at all of when or where the child was born, or when, where and how it died. No documented evidence or anything else to support the claim. Given the incredible detail in the book of all the trivia, it is amazing that there is so little about the one important matter mentioned. Harrison described Ellen Ternan as an Autolycus. My view is that if there was an Autolycus anywhere in the whole saga, it is Gladys Storey. There will be a fuller analysis in a later chapter of what Storey wrote in her book.

So, after that rather disappointing start, all I had was some completely unsubstantiated hearsay about a sexual relationship and the birth and death of an illegitimate child. But upon this incredibly flimsy base, a whole industry of Dickensian scholarship has been founded, with professional and amateur scholars alike all trying desperately to be the one who can find the proof. So far, all that exists are opinions about what has been found and talked about since 1857; every snippet of information being interpreted in such a way as to 'prove', or at least support, the veracity of the Wright/Storey narrative. Anything that may have shed some light on the relationship, but which was written prior to 1857, has been ignored, along with anything which might indicate a contrary view. I have not found, in all the published literature, one person that has asked that very basic question, 'Are there any other explanations that could account for what we are observing?'

As far as possible I shall try to avoid being influenced by what has been written by other commentators in the past, whom, I fear, have been far too greatly influenced by Thomas Wright of Olney, and by Gladys Storey. Thus, I shall try to ignore much of what has been written by others, and simply form my own interpretations of what I can gather from Dickens's own words, that is, from his letters and his fiction. But perhaps I shall use some of the criteria used by others to identify the snippets they then interpret. Because Ellen existed for some eighteen years prior to 1857, I shall start not in that year when every other commentator has started, but in the days before Dickens was married, and work my way through to Ellen's death. I hope to take you along this journey with me, forming an unbiased interpretation as we progress.

Because no one has ever looked for any alternative explanation for what is known, I believe there is a very real possibility that the early commentators such as William Thackeray simply got hold of the wrong end of the stick in 1858. That stick has since passed through successive generations of biographers and commentators like a relay baton, who have used it as a club with which to beat Ellen around the head for over 160 years. I believe that Ellen could well be a totally innocent and blameless young woman; a victim rather than the villain she has been made out to be. I shall now pick up the feather duster and use it to try to brush away the calumnies that have been heaped upon Ellen to reveal a different, untarnished portrait of this much maligned young woman. Very clearly, there was a close relationship between Dickens and Ellen Ternan. All that is known leads one to that conclusion. However, none of what is written really tells us anything about the *nature* of that relationship.

Before I start sweeping, I will make a few comments on my views of Dickens as a writer. His novels are populated with something of the order of 1,500 characters. Some, such as David Copperfield, get a whole book, whereas others get barely a line. One of my favourite characters appears very briefly in *Dombey and Son*. Baby Paul has just been born and Mr Dombey instructs one of the attendants to take Paul to the Nursery:

> 'I'll go down. I'll go down. I needn't beg you,' he added, pausing for a moment at the settee before the fire, 'to take particular care of this young gentleman, Mrs —'
>
> 'Blockitt, Sir?' suggested the nurse, a simpering piece of faded gentility, who did not presume to state her name as a fact, but merely offered it as a mild suggestion.

So very few words, but what a lovely picture they paint of Mrs Blockitt.

At the other end of this spectrum, I will include here an extract from his short story *A Flight*, in which he undertakes a train journey from London to Paris. First published in *Household Words* on 30 August 1851, it was later included in *Reprinted Pieces* in 1858. I shall refer to this story again later because I think it is significant. At this stage of his life Dickens loved the fast travel of the newly established train network. Not at all fast compared to today's high-speed rail reaching speeds upwards of 200 km per hour, but at that time, certainly terrifyingly fast when compared with the alternative horse and carriage.

> Ah! The fresh air is pleasant after the forcing-frame, though it does blow over these interminable streets, and scatter the smoke of this vast wilderness of chimneys. Here we are – no, I mean there we were, for it has darted far into the rear – in Bermondsey where the tanners live. Flash! The distant shipping in the Thames is gone. Whirr! The little streets of new brick and red tile, with here and there a flagstaff growing like a tall weed out

of the scarlet beans, and, everywhere, plenty of open sewer and ditch for the promotion of the public health, have been fired off in a volley. Whizz! Dust-heaps, market-gardens, and waste grounds. Rattle! New Cross Station. Shock! There we were at Croydon. Bur-r-r-r! The tunnel. I wonder why it is that when I shut my eyes in a tunnel I begin to feel as if I were going at an Express pace the other way. I am clearly going back to London now. Compact Enchantress must have forgotten something, and reversed the engine. No! After long darkness, pale fitful streaks of light appear. I am still flying on for Folkestone. The streaks grow stronger – become continuous – become the ghost of day – become the living day – became I mean – the tunnel is miles and miles away, and here I fly through sunlight, all among the harvest and the Kentish hops. There is a dreamy pleasure in this flying. I wonder where it was, and when it was, that we exploded, blew into space somehow, a Parliamentary Train, with a crowd of heads and faces looking at us out of cages, and some hats waving. Monied Interest says it was at Reigate Station. Expounds to Mystery how Reigate Station is so many miles from London, which Mystery again develops to Compact Enchantress. There might be neither a Reigate nor a London for me, as I fly away among the Kentish hops and harvest. What do I care. Bang! We have let another Station off, and fly away regardless. Everything is flying. The hop-gardens turn gracefully towards me, presenting regular avenues of hops in rapid flight, then whirl away. So do the pools and rushes, haystacks, sheep, clover in full bloom delicious to the sight and smell, corn-sheaves, cherry-orchards, apple-orchards, reapers, gleaners, hedges, gates, fields that taper off into little angular corners, cottages, gardens, now and then a church. Bang, bang! A double-barrelled Station! Now a wood, now a bridge, now a landscape, now a cutting, now a – Bang! a single-barrelled Station – there was a cricket-match somewhere with two white tents, and then four flying cows, then turnips – now the wires of the electric telegraph are all alive, and spin, and blurr their edges, and go up and down, and make the intervals between each other most irregular: contracting and expanding in the strangest manner. Now we slacken. With a screwing, and a grinding, and a smell of water thrown on ashes, now we stop.

Here we have an absolutely relentless torrent of words, necessary to convey the rush and bustle of a very fast train ride. So Dickens determines how many words and what sort of punctuations are necessary to convey his thoughts to his audience. While these extracts are from his fictions, which of course were meant to be read by everyone, I think the same is true of his letters, each written to be read only by the addressee. And in those letters, it is frequently the case that very significant statements are made with very few words, sometimes included in long wordy letters. I shall refer to such letters later.

I also want here to mention my approach to interpreting his writing. When it comes to his fictions, I believe it is appropriate to ask oneself what Dickens might have meant by his use of certain phrases, and a little latitude might occasionally be allowed in interpretation. On the other hand, in his private letters, intended only for the eyes of the addressee, I think it is more reasonable to believe that he used the words exactly as they were commonly understood to mean. We must also note that Dickens's writing career started with his brilliant sketches of what he saw around him; of the sights, sounds and smells of London. I believe that when he progressed to writing his more fictional short stories and major novels, he continued to use the same descriptive skills, and wove the sketches into the fabric of the stories to provide the environment in which the characters lived and worked. His characters are, for the most part, 'synthesised' from fragments of a whole range of people he had met, or had at least encountered somewhere through his life.

Now, I might have got this all wrong, but that is how I see it, and that is why I think it is not unreasonable to say that most of Dickens's writing comprises sketches based on his lived experiences woven into his stories. That is not to say that I think everything he wrote was actually autobiographical in the usual sense of the word, rather that we could reasonably expect to find pointers or clues indicating people, places and events he had encountered, even though they had not actually involved him as an immediate participant. And we could anticipate that such pointers and clues could be found in the smaller clusters of words just as well as in the larger passages. And in his letters, I think, he meant exactly what he wrote.

Chapter One

A Very Brief Biography of Charles Dickens, Up to 1857

'NOW, what I want is, Facts. Teach these boys and girls nothing but Facts. Facts alone are wanted in life. Plant nothing else, and root out everything else. You can only form the minds of reasoning animals upon Facts: nothing else will ever be of any service to them. This is the principle on which I bring up my own children, and this is the principle on which I bring up these children. Stick to Facts, sir!'

Charles Dickens; *Hard Times*

****

Following that edict from Mr Gradgrind, I shall here stick to known facts. As far as is possible, I shall not include any other biographer's interpretations or opinions about those facts; just the very straightforward facts. This will be a much abbreviated biography of Charles Dickens, providing only the necessary outline to appreciate the context of his relationship with Ellen Ternan. There are some excellent biographies available, far too many to list here, but which include those by John Forster (1873), Edgar Johnson (1952) Angus Wilson (1970), Peter Ackroyd (1990), Michael Slater

(2009), and Claire Tomalin (2012). More recent biographies are *The Mystery of Charles Dickens* by A.N. Wilson (2020), and one with the tantalising title *The Life and Lies of Charles Dickens* by Helena Kelly (2023), published by Pegasus Books New York, both of which provide some new interpretations of various descriptions of events in Dickens's life. Kelly's book is a refreshingly interesting volume, and very worth reading. However, she does remain steadfast in her adherence to the Wright/Storey narrative as far as Ellen is concerned, and apart from suggesting a possible candidate for the 'baby who died', sheds no new light on the relationship between Dickens and Ellen. With so many biographies readily available it is unnecessary for me to provide anything but the basics which are needed for this little book.

Charles Dickens was born at No. 387, Commercial Road, Landport, Portsea, on Friday, 7 February, 1812. He was the second child of John Dickens, a clerk (with a tendency toward profligacy) in the Navy Pay Office, and his wife Elizabeth, née Barrow. They had a family of eight children, two of whom died in childhood. The first-born was a daughter, Frances (Fanny) (1810–1848). Charles (1812–1870), the first son, was next, followed by Alfred Allen (b and d 1814); Letitia, (1816–1893); Harriet, (1819–1822); Frederick, (1820–1868); Alfred Lamert, (1822–1860); and Augustus (1827–1866).

The very first words written about Charles Dickens appeared in the local Portsmouth newspaper which reported: 'On Friday, at Mile-End Terrace, the Lady of John Dickens esq., a son.' From that humble announcement, as we know, Charles Dickens went on to become, in the opinion of most commentators, one of the best, if not *the* best writer, in the

English language since William Shakespeare. Dickens went on to write fifteen major novels, dozens of short stories and sketches, and articles on all manner of subjects. He also wrote something of the order of 15 - 20,000 letters, many of which are available in the public domain, in a wonderful twelve-volume set referred to as *The Pilgrim Edition,* and which are indeed a very valuable source of information about Dickens and his life, used by all biographers. A complete set of the major works of Dickens occupies about one metre of shelf space in a library – depending on the edition held. On the other hand, books *about* Dickens, occupy about 40 metres of shelf space in the library at Monash University, and I know for a fact that that is an incomplete collection. New biographies are being added every year, some very large scholarly works, others much smaller papers in the learned journals and so on. Most of the content for all those biographies comes from his novels and from his letters, along with 'reminiscences' found in the letters and diaries of a few of his contemporaries. Plus, of course, the interpretations and opinions of each of the biographers. One wonders how much more could be written, but after 400 years, people are still finding more to write about William Shakespeare, so with only 212 years passing since the birth of Dickens, there is every reason to expect that a lot more remains to be written. In 2012, the bicentenary of the birth of Charles Dickens, there was a flurry of new releases, and it was said then that no one could ever have the last word about Dickens. I hope that this small contribution will add something actually worth saying.

His childhood was disrupted, with the family moving from Portsmouth to London, then on to Chatham in Kent by the time he was 5, residing there until he was 11. Chatham was where he first went to school, and it was also where he, with his exceptional powers of observation, absorbed his earliest impressions of humanity, to be subsequently made available as material for his inimitable sketches. He was later to say that the time he spent at Chatham was the happiest of his life.

After Chatham the family finally moved back to London, but his formal education was still somewhat disorganised by his being required to work in some capacity in a blacking factory while his father was incarcerated for a few months in the Marshalsea prison for debt. However, that short period came to an end and he was enrolled at Wellington House Academy, which he attended for a couple of years. He eventually entered the workforce as a clerk in a law office, followed by stints as a court reporter, parliamentary reporter and general journalist. It was through these experiences that he formed his opinions of the law and lawyers, of Government and of politicians, all good grist to his mill, later to find its way into his novels and short stories.

Dickens began his fiction writing career at about age 21, commencing with *A Dinner at Poplar Walk* (1833) for which he received no payment, but much joy and satisfaction. This was later renamed *Mr Minns and His Cousin* for inclusion in a bound edition of *Sketches By Boz,* most of which had initially appeared as items in newspapers as short word-sketches of people and places in and around various parts of London. For these 'sketches' he was paid, and they also made the name Boz a household word. Also at this time, he was 'courting' the pretty young Maria, a daughter of a Mr and Mrs Beadnell. However, after pursuing her for about three years and getting nowhere,

Charles believed that Maria had treated him rather shabbily and that belief, together with some very unhelpful interference from one of Maria's friends, led to the relationship failing to thrive. It was also the case that Mrs Beadnell considered the young Charles Dickens as being not quite the sort of young man for her daughter, being totally unaware at the time that he was in fact the famous Boz. So, just as his writing career started to gain traction, the romance with Maria Beadnell came to an end (May 1833), and we can see from the last letters he sent to her that he believed himself to have been wronged, and he would never be able to forget that.

In a letter dated 18 March 1833 to Maria,[7] Dickens writes of her heartless indifference and of his wretchedness and misery, while claiming to have acted fairly, intelligibly and honourably throughout their intercourse. Thus, in this letter one can see how Dickens is laying the blame squarely on Maria, while delivering his extremely strident defence of his own impeccable behaviour. That he might have said or done something to upset Maria obviously never occurred to him.... 'If (*I can hardly believe it possible*) I have said anything......'

Dickens always had to be right, had to be in control, and others must bend to his will. But Maria did not bend, she left him to go her own wild way and eventually married a banker by the name of Winter. That would have stung him very hard indeed.

He also refers in this letter to the difficulty he will have in forgetting her. This storing up of matters he considered as wrongs done to him, and his inability to forget them is to be a recurring theme throughout his life as we shall see. In another letter to Maria,[8] a couple of months after the one quoted above, he writes, inter alia: 'no consideration on earth shall induce me ever to forget or forgive Fanny's [his sister] not telling me of it before'.

And on the same subject, he wrote on 16 May 1833,[9] again inter alia: 'and if I were to live a hundred years I never would forgive it'.

It is interesting to note that after his father had been released from the Marshalsea, while his father was more than willing for young Charles to discontinue his employment at the blacking factory and return to school, his mother was very keen for him to continue working there. Later, according to Forster, Dickens was to say:[10] 'I never shall forget, I never can forget, that my mother was warm for my being sent back.' Never to forget or forgive. Over and over again, this expression comes up indicating a deeply rooted part of Dickens's character.

Using the pen-name Boz, his identity was not known by the general public until *Pickwick Papers*, coming out at monthly instalments, was about two-thirds complete. *Pickwick Papers* was originally intended to be a more rural, sporty equivalent of the city sketches, the plan being that the well-established artist Robert Seymour would paint pictures of 'Sporting Gentlemen', and Dickens would write the stories to go with them. Dickens agreed, but only on the condition that he would write the stories first, and then he would tell Seymour which scenes he wanted illustrated. Even at this age, at the very start of his career, it became clear that it was to be 'his way or no way', and Seymour, who was his superior in respect of age and, at the time, reputation, reluctantly gave in to Dickens – unlike Maria, who refused. This trait is evident throughout Dickens's life, and in most things he did, he definitely needed to be in control. It might well have been a reaction against his father, who was in control of nothing! Mr John Dickens was certainly not in control of his spending habits, which landed him in the Marshalsea debtor's prison, and young Charles in the blacking factory. Even his job in the Naval Pay Office, which would certainly have given a person some degree of financial stability, actually meant that he was sent to wherever the office needed him to go, rather than to where he might have chosen for himself. This lack of control on the part of Mr Dickens had affected the very young Charles in as much as he was wrenched away from Chatham – a place where Dickens himself later said he had spent the happiest time of his entire life – and had placed him in lodgings in London while the rest of the family were living in the prison with his father. If that period taught the young Charles anything, it was to be prudent with money, and to be in control of your own life.

Almost 'on the rebound', after the romance with Maria Beadnell collapsed, Dickens began his courtship of Catherine Hogarth, the eldest daughter of Scottish lawyer George Hogarth. Hogarth had been a journalist for the *Edinburgh Courant*, and later became a writer and music critic for the *Morning Chronicle*, eventually becoming the editor of the *Evening Chronicle*.

With his now rising fame, and the greatly increased income he was receiving from the sales of *Pickwick Papers*, the new romance blossomed; they became engaged in May 1835, and were married on 2 April 1836. But even before they were married, his letters to Catherine began to indicate his need to direct and to 'form her mind' to suit him, and it seems that he was easily upset. In late May, within three weeks of becoming engaged to Catherine, something – though it is far from clear what – induced him to write to her[11] complaining about her sudden and uncalled-for coldness and seeking explanations for it. He accuses her of trifling with him, of using him like a toy and teasing him, and he demands that whatever has caused her to act in this way must be overcome. This letter appears to carry the same message as those to Maria. That is, Dickens has behaved impeccably, so the cause of her coldness and sullenness must lie within Catherine herself, and it was her responsibility to overcome it. And again, that indication that it could never be forgotten.

Throughout their engagement they exchanged many letters. There are some sixty letters to Catherine written between their getting engaged in May 1835 and being married in April 1836, and with the exception of the one above, most are very loving. Many are quite short, and include apologies for his not being able to meet with her due to the pressures of his work. It is also interesting to see how often he was troubled with headaches, colds and pains in his side. It appears that he was working very long hours during this time with late-night sittings of parliament, late theatre trips (for the purpose of writing a review for the next morning's papers), and travelling to outlying towns for general reporting duties. This was all in addition to his commitment to providing the next *Sketch* in the series and starting work on *Pickwick Papers*. Throughout his life Dickens was a ferociously hard worker and was frequently plagued by various ailments.

After their marriage, Catherine's younger sister Mary came to stay with them as a companion for Catherine – a practice quite common in the first half of the nineteenth century. The relationship between Dickens and Mary has been written about ad nauseam, and most commentators generally tell the same story, but it is interesting to note that Forster doesn't mention Mary at all. He does not mention that she came to live with the newly wedded Charles and Catherine, nor that she died suddenly at the age of 18, and that Dickens was so distraught at her death that he took a ring from her finger and wore it for the rest of his life. Apparently, he also kept some of her clothes. Similarly, G.K. Chesterton doesn't mention her in his 1903 *Biography of Dickens*, but by 1933 she is beginning to be quite widely included. Bernard Darwin, in his biography of Dickens for a series of Great Lives,[12] is quite clear about the relationship between Dickens and Mary Hogarth both prior to, and following, her death. This is the earliest book I have found in which Mary Hogarth's contribution to Dickens's writing is explored, and possibly could be considered one of the first in the twentieth century genre of psychography. Forster would have known about the sudden death of Mary, and of any significant reaction that Dickens might have had at that time. Either he deliberately wrote her out, or he did not attach any importance to her.

Earlier biographers concentrated on describing the 'whats' 'wheres' and 'whens' of their subject's lives. Post Sigmund Freud, biographers became more interested in the 'whys' and the 'consequences'. Forster was an 'old school' biographer, really providing not much more than a narrative based on geography, actions and time. A new school of artistic criticism, pioneered in France by Charles Augustin Sainte-Beuve (1804–1869) but not used by Forster, worked on the theory that 'to understand the art, it was necessary to understand the artist'.

But how do you get to know and understand an artist after they have died and are no longer available for in-depth interviews? Enter Sigmund Freud. Biographers started using Freudian theory to 'understand' the artist. The first British follower of this school was Lytton Strachey (1880–1932) followed by Gamaliel Bradford (1866–1932) in America, and they started writing 'psychographies' and 'psychobiographies'. However, despite their large output, neither ever wrote a biography of Charles Dickens.

Taking the case of Mary Hogarth, Dickens portrayed her as Rose Maylie possibly because he was distraught at her death just after he started writing *Oliver Twist*. As he was unable to gratify his apparent obsession with Mary in life, he reinvented her as the many young women depicted in his fictions. From that time, this frequent portrayal of young women in his novels was then interpreted as Dickens being obsessed with 18-year-olds in general. However, the fictional 18-year-olds didn't really cut the mustard for him, which was later used to explain his then being infatuated with one Christiana Weller (an 18-year-old pianist). However, he got no more gratification from that direction, when Christiana upped and married his friend T.J. Thompson. So he continued with the fictional 18-year-olds until he found Ellen Ternan (or so the analysis goes), and later eventually being gratified in real life with, in his mind, a living reincarnation of Mary. So, the process appears to be that you look for something in the man to explain the art, then use that something in the art to explain the man. That all seems a little cyclic to my mind. It is also interesting to note that as already mentioned Forster said nothing of Ellen other than to quote Dickens's will, and G.K. Chesterton mentioned neither

Mary nor Ellen at all. Darwin writes extensively of Mary as being the progenitor of several of Dickens's heroines, but his only mention of Ellen is in relation to the 'Violated Letter' and takes the form 'Of the "young lady" it is enough to say that she was Miss Ellen Ternan, who had acted once or twice with Dickens. He left her £1,000 in his will. There is no scrap of evidence to show that Dickens's words about her were not absolutely true.'

But of course, Forster, Chesterton and Darwin were writing well before the publication of the books of Wright and Storey, and therefore had not been tainted by their claims about Ellen.

But in the case of Ellen, two spokes in the cyclic interpretation wheel were Thomas Wright and Gladys Storey (1935 and 1939 respectively), with their unsubstantiated claims. But of course as they fitted well with the more carnal than psychological explanations, and therefore easier to believe, their narrative became the 'accepted truth'. But after all is said and done, it comes down to opinions based on psychoanalytic theory rather than evidence. As W.H. Auden said in his *In Memory of Sigmund Freud*, Freud created a whole climate of opinion under whom we conduct our different lives.

Within two weeks of their marriage, probably while still on honeymoon at the village of Chalk near the Medway towns of Chatham and Rochester, Catherine became pregnant, and their first child, Charles Culliford Boz, was born on 6 January 1837. As was very much the practice at that time, Catherine would be 'confined' for up to four weeks post-partum, and through that time she suffered dreadfully with post-natal depression. This depression would be repeated for the next three births, (Mary, 1838; Katey, 1839; Walter, 1841) but eventually, when Dickens realised that 'confinement' was much more of a custom than a medical necessity, Catherine was allowed to re-enter the family life much sooner following her subsequent deliveries, and her suffering was greatly reduced. But here again, it appears to have been Dickens, rather than Catherine, who made the decision not to continue with the customary confinements.

Very soon after Catherine was released from her confinement following Charles's birth, she was pregnant again, but the sudden and unexpected death of her sister Mary (7 May 1837) mentioned above, may well have been a factor contributing to the miscarriage of that child. Dickens was also very distraught, more at the loss of Mary Hogarth it seems, than at the loss of Catherine's child. In order to escape, in the first week of July Dickens decided to take Catherine to Northern France for a break, along with his illustrator, Hablot Browne. By the time they returned from France, or at least within a few days after that return, Catherine was pregnant again, this time going the full term with Mary (known as 'Mamie' within the family), born 6 March 1838. At about this stage, Catherine's younger sister, 15-year-old Georgina, came to stay, again with a view to her being a companion and help-mate to Catherine. This 'visit' continued until Dickens's death in 1870.

To aid Catherine's recovery from the birth of Mary, Dickens rented accommodation for the family outside of London in the cleaner, leafier parts of Twickenham and Petersham. Dickens himself commuted between their London house in Doughty Street, and the rural lodgings, spending a few days at each place on rotation.

Having looked at a few of the letters written by Dickens, from which we can get a glimpse of the man himself at this time, let us turn to his fictions thus far, from 1833 to 1838. The *Sketches* were, for the most part, descriptions of sights, smells and sounds he had experienced in and around London. Sketches of the people he had passed in the streets, seen in the shops, in the places of his day jobs as a clerk in a legal office, and as a court and a parliamentary reporter. All written brilliantly and, importantly, all from his lived experience. When he was invited to write sketches to go with illustrations of humorous sporting situations already made by Seymour, he accepted the commission subject to his writing the stories first, and asking Seymour to then illustrate particular events that Dickens had described, rather than the other way round. That would have given Dickens the freedom to write about subjects and situations with which he was already familiar, in his own way – the way he knew he could achieve the best outcome for all. If we look at *Pickwick Papers*, it starts with the cabbies in London, moves to the Medway towns, includes a military pageant and mock battle, back to London, an election, the trial of Bardel vs Pickwick, and Mr Pickwick's incarceration in the Marshalsea debtor's prison, to pick out just a few examples. These are all parts of Dickens's lived experiences. Before he even completes *Pickwick*, he starts writing *Oliver Twist*, again describing much of what he had experienced as a lad working in the blacking factory, walking the streets alone at night, seeing the other urchins roaming round the seedier parts of town. Again, much of the descriptions and emotions coming from his lived experience.

In light of the suggestion that much of Dickens's early writing seems to include – if not originate in – his lived experience, should we expect his later writing to similarly include clues to parts of his life that are perhaps not so obvious as the Marshalsea and the blacking factory?

Following *Oliver Twist* there is *Nicholas Nickleby*, with Nicholas's financially imprudent, albeit late, father, and his joining the Crummles family of travelling players. It is known that even during his time in an office, Dickens had seriously considered a career on the stage, and had it not been for an illness striking at the precise time of his audition, he might well have become a professional actor and part-time amateur author, rather than the other way round. However, I shall not go through all of Dickens's novels at this stage because I shall do that in a later chapter.

The period of Dickens's life, from his marriage in 1836 to 1852 – six years prior to his separation from Catherine – was incredibly productive both family-wise and in a literary sense. Through those sixteen years Dickens fathered ten children with Catherine, starting while on their honeymoon, with Charles Culliford Boz, through to Edward Bulwer Lytton in 1852. Sixteen years. Some 190 months. Ten full-term pregnancies and at least one, maybe two, miscarriages. Assuming the full-term pregnancies each lasted the standard 9.5 months, and the two miscarriages were one to two months each, it makes a total of about ninety-eight months out of the 190. Just about 52 per cent of Catherine's life through that time was spent in a state of pregnancy. And to that one could add the periods of post-natal depression.

It is no wonder that at times Catherine was tired to the point of being considered indolent, and that she put on a lot of weight. She was, after all, eating for two for more than half of her married life up to 1852. The rapidity with which Dickens re-impregnated Catherine following each birth might be an indication of his libido. According to Lillian Nayder,[13] and based on a statement he made about not eating oysters for a while, Dickens may well have ceased intercourse for the last trimester of each pregnancy, and he certainly appeared to resume normality on Catherine's recovery from any post-natal depression.

It is also possible that he did occasionally seek the services of prostitutes. This assumption comes from a letter he wrote to his friend Maclise[14] while holidaying at Broadstairs, inviting him to join with the family there. In this letter Dickens referred to 'all kinds of conveniences', and 'I know where they live'. Tomalin[15] expressed her doubt that he would have been referring to the donkeys on the beach; rather, she believes he was writing of the local brothels. Further indications of Dickens possibly having consorted with prostitutes are to be found in his defence of the poet Samuel Rogers who was charged with exploiting a prostitute many years earlier. Dickens pointed out that prostitutes were willing and consenting parties and went on to say, 'Good God if such sins were to be visited upon all of us and to hunt us down through life, what man would escape.'[16] There is also a suggestion that he might have contracted gonorrhoea, probably from a prostitute. This is suggested in a letter[17] dated 16 August 1859 to Wilkie Collins, referring to 'perhaps a tumble in the sea might – but I suppose there is no nitrate of silver in the ocean?' For a brief period in the nineteenth century, silver nitrate was used as a treatment for gonorrhoea.

The fact that Catherine spent so much of her time being pregnant might also excuse her from the later charges of abandoning her children to the ever-faithful sister Georgina. To be honest, I think it would have been more surprising had she managed to cope without the help of Georgina – and after all, that was the reason why Georgina was staying there, with free board and lodgings, clothes, holidays and other living expenses all paid from Dickens's purse. It seems to me that the stallion Dickens was simply seeing Catherine as a brood mare, and I think she has been very unjustly criticised. After the birth of one child he apparently wrote, 'My wife has presented me with another child; an honour I could have done without.' I get the impression that Dickens believed she was delivering him children as presents on the scale of the gifting immortalised in the song *The Twelve Days of Christmas*.

While breeding so prolifically, his quill pen was equally busy. As well as completing eight major novels he made extended trips to America and to Italy, both resulting in travel books, (*American Notes* and *Pictures from Italy*), wrote five Christmas Books, and *A Child's History of England*. In addition to his writing, he was also heavily involved in the establishment and running of Urania Cottage (a Home for Homeless Women, largely funded by the banking heiress Angela Burdett-Coutts). He was involved in other activities too numerous to list here, but generally of a philanthropic nature.

His breeding ended with the birth of Edward Bulwer Lytton in 1852, but his writing continued unabated, and by 1858 Dickens had completed three more novels, (*Bleak House, Hard Times* and *Little Dorrit*). He was running himself ragged, but also embarked on a number of readings of his own works, given in aid of various worthy causes. These met with such success that he started to seriously consider giving a series of readings for his own benefit. His parents and other various relatives were still a drain on his purse, as was his ever-growing family, including the sister-in-law, Georgina. He was also considering purchasing Gad's Hill Place, near Rochester in Kent, a house he had much admired as a child. He discussed his plans for a series of readings with his friend Forster, who was dead set against it on two heads. First, Forster was concerned for Dickens's health, and second, Forster considered that public readings of his works for money would be an insult to the higher art of writing.

For relaxation, or at least for a break from the family duties, he was an avid theatre-goer, a passion which had started as a child building model theatres for amusement. He also made extended summer holidays with the family at places such as Broadstairs, across the English Channel at Boulogne, and further afield such as Paris and Switzerland, and would also make extended trips away with male friends including Wilkie Collins and Augustus Egg. To sum it all up, he was rarely, if ever, idle. It seemed as though he had unlimited energy, and frequently spent some of the excess taking long very brisk walks. It is also interesting to see how frequently he dined with groups of his male friends which included several actors, painters and other writers.

And so his life steamed on at full speed, until it hit a very bumpy track at Manchester in 1857. Following a three-day season of the Wilkie Collins play, *The Frozen Deep*, given by Dickens's group of amateur actors in aid of a fund for the widow and daughter of his deceased friend Douglas Jerrold, lives were to change forever. At that moment, to mix the metaphors, the wheels came off and it all went very pear-shaped – and Ellen was to be one of the casualties.

Before we go into the details of the disaster, it is of interest to note that Dickens had been anticipating some circumstance from his past reemerging and causing him difficulties. Shortly after *The Frozen Deep* performances he wrote to Forster a quite lengthy letter, included in Forster's 1873 *Life of Dickens* which contained this short statement, of the sort I mentioned earlier; brief, but very significant: 'What is befalling me now, I have seen coming since the days you remember when Mary was born.'

But when whatever it was that he had seen coming actually arrived, it was to be much more damaging and problematical than he had envisaged!

So let us now turn back the clock to 1838, and to the all-important days when Mary was born.

Chapter Two

Ellen Grows Up

All the world's a stage, and all the men and women merely players. They have their entrances and their exits; and one man in his time plays many parts....
William Shakespeare (*As You Like It*)

As discussed in the introduction, there was clearly a very strong and close relationship between Charles Dickens and Ellen Ternan. However, because of the impact of Wright and Storey, with the later strident support of Ada Nisbet,[18] all those scholars, professional and amateur alike who have since commented on the business started with the premise that there was a child (of necessity including a sexual relationship), and started their research from 1857 when Dickens and Ellen acted together in *The Frozen Deep*. Those who sought to disagree only tried to point out the failings and shortcomings of the Wright/Storey narrative, trying to discredit them, but without attempting to formulate any other narrative that could explain what was actually known. My intention here is to put forward a narrative that accounts for all of the known facts, taking into account Ellen's existence for eighteen years prior to 1857 – a fact which appears to have been totally ignored by just about everybody in their attempts to find the proof for the Wright/Storey narrative. Inclusion of those earlier years of Ellen's life makes it reasonable to consider the alternative possibility that the relationship between Dickens and Ellen was filial, rather than carnal.

From the brief biography in the previous chapter, you will see that during June/July 1838, Catherine Dickens was recuperating at Twickenham from the birth of daughter Mary while Charles Dickens was largely back at Doughty Street in London. During this time, he was frequently attending theatre performances, just as he regularly did throughout his life. One of the closest theatres to Doughty Street was the Theatre Royal at Drury Lane, a matter of about one kilometre, and it would not be unreasonable, in fact it would be highly probable, that he would have attended performances there as well as at other theatres. At that time, Mrs Frances Ternan, née Jarman, was performing quite regularly with Charles Kean at the Theatre Royal as indicated by theatre notices in local newspapers. Given that Mrs Ternan was well known to Dickens's friend the actor and theatre manager William Macready, it is equally probable that he knew of Frances Ternan even if he had not at that time met her personally. Ellen was born in March 1839, and assuming a standard thirty-nine-week gestation, counting back from that date puts her conception in mid-late June 1838. Is it reasonable to make a connection between Charles Dickens and Ellen Ternan even at this very embryonic stage? I certainly believe it is worth looking at, and here I shall grab at a straw floating in a biography of Dickens by Angus Wilson, a very staunch ally of Ada Nisbet. Wilson opines that Ellen could, in age, so well have been his daughter.[19]

Now why did Wilson not even investigate that last possibility? The answer to that, of course, was his very strong belief in the

Wright/Storey narrative that was so strenuously supported by Ada Nisbet. I also believe that the precautions Dickens took to hide the relationship and the degree to which Ellen herself felt the need for this would be just as strong whether Ellen was his illegitimate daughter or his mistress. Certainly Ellen would not wish it to be known that she was illegitimate, and that her mother was an adulteress. I will add here an extract from Peter Ackroyd's *Dickens*. Ackroyd, who is one of the few biographers to doubt the Wright/Storey narrative, concludes from his research that it was unlikely that the relationship between Dickens and Ellen was consummated. But he still needed to give an explanation for Dickens's behaviour, and to account for why Dickens was so secretive about it. Rather than being wedded to the Wright/Storey narrative as most other biographers have been, Ackroyd appears to have sought the aid of the psychoanalyst, Sigmund Freud. This, from Ackroyd:[20] 'There have been many speculations about the exact nature of the relationship between Dickens and Ellen in this period ... (all variations on the Wright/Storey narrative) ... It has to be said at once that *no evidence has ever been found for any of these more dramatic possibilities...* [my emphasis].'

Ackroyd then goes on to try to answer the question 'what was their relationship?', and to do so he raises the question of Dickens's relationship with Mary Hogarth, and with Christiana Weller. He also refers to the sexless passion between brother and sister or between adult and child frequently cropping up in his novels and short stories. He then refers to the playful relationship between Bella Wilfer and her father. From all of this, which occupies about four pages of psychography, he concludes that it was most unlikely that the relationship between Dickens and Ellen was a consummated affair and sums it up thus: 'The whole parade of his heroines might come to this, then – this sexless marriage between brother and sister, or father and daughter.'

I am not a psychologist looking into people's minds. Rather I was an electron-microscopist, simply dealing with what I could see, albeit that viruses are incredibly small; maybe that is why I am drawn to take more notice of Dickens's very brief, but very informative statements; looking for the smallest of details. While it is clear that Ackroyd is trying to get away from the standard Wright/Storey narrative, it seems rather a convoluted route to reach the point of thinking about a father/daughter relationship between Dickens and Ellen. You do not need to go through all the Freudian psychoanalysis of sexless marriages with idealised virgins. You simply need to ask the question, if she was not his mistress, if it was not simply platonic, could it not perhaps be simply filial, a common or garden father/daughter relationship, already mentioned by Angus Wilson, and here, as in the case of Bella and her father, suggested by Ackroyd?

Having sown the seed of an idea that Ellen was the daughter, not the mistress, of Charles Dickens, I shall leap forward to 2000, and the publication of an article[21] by Professor John Bowen in which he interprets the story of Bebelle in *His Boot*s. This was one of the short stories included in the Christmas Story of 1862 with the overall title of *Somebody's Luggage*. ('All the Year Round' 1862). The thinking behind the complete set of *Somebody's Luggage* was that a locked suitcase was left at a lodging place by a visitor with the message: 'To be held until called for'. After several years had passed, the owner of the lodging decided that quite clearly the owner of the luggage was not going to return or to call for it, so he might as well open it and see if there were any clues inside as to what he should do with the suitcase. What he found was a suit of clothes, and attached to each garment was a short story, and the story attached to the pair of boots was that of Bebelle. Dickens had the intention that each of the short stories would be contributed by a different author, but as it got close to the deadline he realised that too few were going to contribute, so he had no option other than to write at least two of them himself.

His Boots is set in a coastal town in northern France, possibly Boulogne, where an English gentleman, Monsieur Langlais, has taken up occupancy in an upstairs room overlooking the town square. From this vantage point M. Langlais watches a trooper caring for the needs of the presumed illegitimate toddler Bebelle. Clearly the toddler is very attached to the trooper, and is totally dependent on him for food, clothes, accommodation and companionship. In due course, there is a major fire in the town, and the trooper is killed while helping extinguish the conflagration. The trooper is buried, and M. Langlais finds Bebelle weeping on his grave, with no one available to look after and care for her. Accordingly, M. Langlais, with the help of the local Mayor, M. Mutuel, adopts Bebelle and takes her back to England with him.

In his interpretation of this story, Professor Bowen tries to demonstrate that at this time (1862), Dickens's thoughts were constantly turning to illegitimacy, fatherhood and forgiveness, and this story is therefore linked to the illegitimate child Dickens has fathered with Ellen, and which has (supposedly) just been born and/or died.

However, it is important to note the fact that most of the Bebelle story had been included in letters that Dickens had written to Wilkie Collins,[22] while on holiday in Boulogne in 1854, and to a Mrs Brown.[23] In those letters, Dickens related how he had seen a trooper of the French Military, while waiting for deployment to the Crimea, look after, feed and meet the needs of the toddler child of a senior officer. Those letters also described a fire at a theatre, and the attempts by the military and by the community to extinguish the blaze. Given that Dickens had been let down by other authors and had eventually needed to produce the stories himself at very short notice, it is unsurprising that he should recycle some material he had written several years earlier but which hitherto had not found its way into the public domain. So Bebelle probably has very little to do with Dickens's state of mind in 1862, and is probably not a reflection in fiction of an illegitimate birth in reality at that time. I have previously suggested[24] (in my paper published in *The Dickensian*) that if Dickens was thinking about a small child of his own when writing *His Boots*, it is quite possible that he was thinking back to 1854 (the time in which the whole *Luggage* story is set) when those letters were written, and perhaps thinking of his daughter Dora, who was born on 16 August 1850 and died on 15 April 1851. In 1854 she would have been about the same age as Bebelle had she not died so young. Dickens himself described the story as pretty and very slight in itself, hardly indicating a work of soul-searching significance. It seems that he was more concerned with the accuracy with which he had portrayed its setting, and after *Somebody's Luggage* had been published, Dickens wrote to his business manager Wills[25] expressing his satisfaction with the accuracy with which he had recalled and portrayed the old Northern French towns.

Having said all that, let us suppose that Professor Bowen is correct, and an illegitimacy in Dickens's fiction can indeed be equated with one in his own life. If we follow that train of thought, then we should start the search with *Oliver Twist* (1837–9), and perhaps go on to look more closely at others such as Esther Summerson, Arthur Clennam and Estella – all of whom, like Bebelle, are illegitimate and have that hard E sound in their names. Indeed, I am grateful to Professor Bowen for planting the idea of looking at the other illegitimacies in Dickens's novels to help strengthen the idea of Ellen being his illegitimate daughter. John Bowen noted in his article that there were many other illegitimate characters spread through the novels and short stories, but just as Angus Wilson did not follow up on the idea of Ellen being Dickens's daughter, Bowen also failed to follow it up. I suspect that there were common reasons why both scholars chose to ignore their own thoughts, and those, of course, include the determination to stick with, and to try to provide evidence to support, the Wright/Storey narrative so strongly supported by Ada Nisbet. I also suspect that if *His Boots* had been published at any time other than 1862, it would have passed unremarked.

In order to see if there are any clues at all in Dickens's fiction and his letters to indicate a much earlier relationship with Ellen, I will look at all the young girls and other characters, particularly (but not exclusively) those who are illegitimate, from 1838 to 1857. So let us now look at *Oliver Twist*. (1837–9), where I think Ellen might well have made her first appearance.

At the start of *Oliver Twist* there is only the slightest hint that he is illegitimate. All we know is that his heavily pregnant and very distraught mother makes her way to the workhouse where she dies shortly after giving birth to Oliver, and the Beadle, Mr Bumble, remarks 'The usual story I suppose'. It is not until much later in the novel, after the appearance of the rather mysterious and villainous Monks, that we learn about Oliver's parentage and illegitimacy. This part of the story was written late in 1838, at a time when, according to Peter Ackroyd, Dickens unravelled the mystery of Oliver's parentage, a complicated exercise which he seems to have had to make up as he went along. This was also a time at which, again according to Ackroyd, Dickens appeared to be chaffing against the strains of domesticity – a sense of wishing to break away from bonds … and further, that Dickens's mind seems to have been in turmoil through September/October 1838.

Catherine had given birth to their second child, Mary, on 6 March 1838, and was suffering from postnatal depression. To aid her recovery, the Dickenses had rented accommodation in Twickenham (at that time a rural outer suburb of London), and Catherine stayed there while Charles made frequent trips back to London for work. As mentioned earlier, it is inconceivable that Dickens would have spent time alone in London without going several times to the theatre, and indeed there is a letter to his friend and actor William Macready[26] asking if his name could be added to the list of those who were permitted access to the theatre via the stage door. Dickens claims that he had already entered through that door on at least fifty occasions, but had recently been prevented from so doing by the inebriated doorman. While this letter specifically referred to the Theatre

Royal, Covent Garden, and might well be an exaggeration as to the number of visits made, it certainly indicates that Dickens was not sitting moping at home while Catherine was away. It is not beyond the realms of possibility that on one of those short stays at Doughty Street, Dickens did stray from the straight and narrow, and did have a brief affair with an actress. Dickens became concerned that he might have fathered a child as a result of the affair, and that is why, as Professor Bowen indicated, his thoughts were constantly turning to illegitimacy, fatherhood and forgiveness. And it was that torment that created the difficulty he was experiencing in working out the parentage of Oliver Twist, and why his mind was in turmoil.

Before proceeding further with that line of enquiry, it might be helpful to remember some of the opinions of Lillian Nader, outlined in her book *The Other Dickens; A life of Catherine Hogarth*, mentioned in the previous chapter. Professor Nader pointed out Dickens's possibly using the services of prostitutes in order to satisfy his libido at times when Catherine was pregnant. So, having come to the conclusion, however shaky, that Dickens needed fairly frequent relief for his active libido, the suggestion of his having an affair in June 1838 while Catherine was 'indisposed' should not be ruled out. And after all, if the believers of the standard narrative of the Ellen Ternan saga are so willing to accept that Dickens could have had an affair with an actress at the age of 47, why would it be considered so unlikely that he might have had an affair with an actress at the age of 27? Does Dickens himself give us any other hint as to his activities in mid-1838?

At the end of the previous chapter, I referred to a letter (7 September 1857) that Dickens wrote to Forster shortly after the *Frozen Deep* performances in which he wrote, inter alia, 'what is befalling me now I have seen coming since the days you remember when Mary was born'. In this letter, meant only for the eyes of Forster and not for the general public, why did Dickens think it necessary to mention 'the days you remember'? He could have so easily and simply said 'since Mary was born', or, 'for a long time', and left it at that. Had he said 'for some time', that would have been in accordance with with several letters exchanged between Dickens and his friends at the time of the marriage of Queen Victoria in 1840. These letters, generally interpreted as being high-spirited jokes, are referred to in greater detail in the next chapter, but the gist is that they indicate some marital disharmony between Dickens and Catherine – some two years after Mary was born. Those more general words would also have accorded with the musings of David Copperfield in 1849–50. Under that circumstance, it would be reasonable to believe that Dickens had been anticipating the end of his marriage for some time. But is it likely that the successful birth of a daughter in 1838 following the unsuccessful pregnancy of the previous year would have triggered thoughts of his marriage disintegrating? I think not. So was there something very special and memorable in the days following Mary's birth that he was so keen to remind Forster of? One event that we can be absolutely sure did happen was Mrs Frances Ternan becoming pregnant with Ellen at that time, during the last couple of weeks of June.

As you read those words 'the days you remember', you can almost hear these thoughts (speculation from my very small streak of creativity) going through Dickens's mind....

'The days you remember! Do you remember them, John? Those few days in London? Catherine was at Twickenham convalescing after Mary was born. The theatre every night; the late-night dinners; the fascinating Fanny Ternan that Macready introduced to us? Halcyon days! We knew they couldn't last forever, and they didn't last for long; but the memories stay with you. They haunt you. They haunted me! They affected everything I did, everything I wrote from that time on. I knew that at some time the past would inevitably catch up with me, and the truth would come out.'

It may be a long bow to draw to suggest at this stage that Dickens did have an affair, a youthful dalliance perhaps, a youthful indiscretion maybe, with Mrs Ternan during that time, and that Forster was quite aware of it. But it is by no means beyond the bounds of possibility. I have no traditional 'smoking gun' or the more recent tool of the forensic scientists, DNA on the bed sheets, but we can put Mrs Ternan and Charles Dickens in the same geographical area, within a couple of kilometres, at the same time, while Catherine was away from home.

At the time of writing the last chapters of *Oliver Twist*, Dickens may have had suspicions, perhaps no more than 'gut feelings', that he might have fathered a child, but like Thomas Wright of Olney, at the time had no actual proof. Maybe this could explain the turmoil in Dickens's mind noted by Ackroyd. Anyone who has ever lost a child, for whatever reason and at whatever time in the child's development, goes through the rest of their life wondering what 'might have been' for that child.

Dickens would have been no different, and the child he believed to be his, but which he had never met, continued to push its way into all facets of his life, including his novels and short stories. In light of that possibility, we shall continue to look for other clues in the pre-*Frozen Deep* era of Dickens's novels.

Even before completing *Oliver Twist,* Dickens started work on *Nicholas Nickleby* (1838–9), and introduces the Crummles Family. Mr Crummles, a large heavy man, was an actor–manager of his touring company, which included his wife and three children, one of which was promoted as 'The Infant Phenomenon'. It is largely held that the Crummles family was based on a Mr T.D. Davenport (1792–1851) and his daughter Jean (1829–1903), an infant phenomenon, and as I mentioned in the introduction, Dickens often infused his characters with fragments of the characteristics of living individuals. Thus it is not beyond the realms of possibility that the Crummles family also includes echoes of the Ternan Family, the patriarch Thomas Ternan also being a stout man, the other members at the time being his wife and two daughters, all of whom were actors who toured the provinces.

Returning now to June 1838 (when Ellen was conceived) it was at the very end of June/early July that Mr Ternan moved to Newcastle with his wife, two daughters and Ellen (*in utero*). It was also the time when the first part of the still incomplete *Nicholas Nickleby* was dramatised and being performed in the new Newcastle theatre. The Ternans, acting in *Clari, The Maid of Milan* which was included in the same programme, would almost certainly have seen the Nickleby play. Dickens's description of the Crummles family, a country theatre manager and his family in *Nickleby* was also a pretty good reflection of the Ternans; they even had an 'infant phenomenon' in preparation in little Fanny.

Following the completion of *Nicholas Nickleby* Dickens was supposed to have started work on his 'historical novel' based on the Gordon Riots, *Barnaby Rudge*, for which he had already entered into a contract with his publishers. However, he did not do so immediately, rather he launched a miscellany with the overarching title of *Master Humphrey's Clock*. Master Humphrey, an elderly gentleman with a physical deformity, owned an old Grandfather clock, in the cabinet of which were stored a number of manuscripts of various short stories. The plan for the miscellany was that each week, either Master Humphrey or one of his friends would take a manuscript from the clock and read it to the group as they sat around the fire. The first of these short stories was all about a young girl, Nelly Trent, and told of her becoming lost on the way home from running an errand for her ageing grandfather. She is found by Master Humphrey, who takes her back to the grandfather who runs an old curiosity shop. In this short story we are told nothing of Nelly's parentage, or of the problems of the grandfather, and that is probably how it would have remained but for an opportunistic twist that arose after the next few issues. The issue which included the story of Nelly Trent was very popular, and the magazine sold exceptionally well. However, subsequent editions were not so successful, and it was soon recognised by Dickens that his readers did not want a series of short stories, they would prefer a proper, good length novel. Thus, given the initial popularity of Nelly Trent, Dickens morphed it into the full-length novel *The Old Curiosity Shop*, arguably his most popular novel. In the original short story, the girl was referred to by her grandfather on some occasions as Nell, and on others as Nelly. However, in the resulting book, she is always referred to as Little Nell. It is worth noting that both Nell and Nelly have been commonly used as a diminutive form of the baptismal names Eleanor and Ellen.

Returning to the task of tracking any clues to Ellen Ternan in Dickens's novels prior to 1857, we have here a girl named Nell (Dickens frequently used Nelly for Ellen), and a surname, Trent, as close to Ternan as the pseudonyms Tringham, Turnan and Turnham, supposedly used by Dickens in renting accommodation for Ellen and her mother, about which so much is made. At the time of the writing of *The Old Curiosity Shop* Ellen would have been nearly 2 years old. Through his interest in, and connections with, the theatre, including his friend William Macready who was also well known to the Ternans, Dickens is certain to have been aware of her birth (which incidentally took place at Rochester), and her name. It is far more than a coincidence that he should name this particular character with one so similar if he had been totally unconnected to her. I am not suggesting for a moment that Little Nell *is* the toddler Ellen. The character was apparently built around a child Dickens had seen strolling in the company of an older man in St James's Place, Bath, behind the house at St James Square in which he was staying at the time. But I am suggesting that he chose the name because toddler Ellen was in his mind at that time.

The next illegitimate character is Maypole Hugh, the ostler at the Maypole Inn (*Barnaby Rudge* 1841). Hugh was the illegitimate son of the wealthy Mr (later Sir) John Chester, and a gypsy woman who had later been hanged for petty theft.

While there is nothing directly relating to Dickens's current situation here, it is a reminder that Dickens is still considering the possible outcome of his own indiscretion three years earlier. Sir John of course denied that Hugh was his son, and maybe Dickens was, not so much denying to himself, but perhaps hoping that his gut feeling about baby Ellen Ternan may not be right.

Before we move on to the next illegitimate character, to wit, Esther Summerson (*Bleak House*, 1852–3) it is worth, I think, having a very quick look at *Dombey and Son* (1846–8), and a more detailed look at the 1848 Christmas Book, *The Haunted Man*.

While Florence Dombey is not illegitimate, she has certainly been very much neglected by her father, and it is quite possible that this is also a reflection of Dickens's troubled conscience about neglecting the child he believes he has fathered. It is perhaps also worth noting that Ellen, who was at the time of *Dombey and Son* about the same age as Florence, like her, had a brother (born 1842) who failed to thrive. Admittedly baby Paul Dombey lived a few years longer than the baby Thomas Ternan, but the similarity cannot be ignored, I think. Dickens would almost certainly have been aware of baby Ternan's demise, and was perhaps thinking about Ellen losing her brother while he was working through Florence losing hers.

I want here to have a more detailed look at the 1848 Christmas Book, *The Haunted Man* and also note a few comments from Peter Ackroyd's *Dickens*.

Ellen is now 9 years old, and Dickens is beginning to feel very guilty about the child that might well be his. Even though he was on the Continent staying in Switzerland and France at the time, he would probably have been aware through his theatrical contacts that Mr Ternan had died, and that the Ternan family's future was precarious. It is quite probable that in his troubled conscience, he was even considering the possibility of a destitute Mrs Ternan appearing on his doorstep with the three children, seeking some assistance. He may or may not have been reassured by his friend William Macready, who did step forward to assist Mrs Ternan immediately after the death of her husband, but it is pretty certain that he would have known of her plight.

The Haunted Man tells of Mr Redlaw, haunted and troubled by his memories of past wrong-doings, who makes a deal with his own ghost to wipe out all those unpleasant memories. However, as he is unable to select the specific memories of wrong-doing, all are erased, and he is left with no humanity or compassion in his soul. Worse, he is cursed to pass this affliction on to anyone who comes into contact with him. He is eventually relieved of that part of the curse through the goodness of Milly Swidger, the wife of the lodge keeper in the almost ruined college building in which he lived, but he never regains his own memories despite the motto on the wall to 'Keep my Memory Green'. Clearly Dickens is becoming increasingly troubled by the memory of his wrong-doing, but knows full well that he will never be able to eradicate those memories, and that they will continue to haunt him and populate his novels. He was sure that eventually, the truth will out.

It is worth noting here another comment from *Dickens* by Peter Ackroyd.[27] Ackroyd is writing of the time of Dickens's separation from Catherine and comments that an unnamed source had mentioned that Dickens never seemed to be at ease, and always seemed to have something on his mind as well as in it.

I cannot help thinking that in *The Haunted Man*, we are seeing that 'something on his mind' – the memories of a wrong done at some time in the past that are now haunting him. And as we have already seen, Dickens was never able to forget what he considered to be a wrong done by others, and that most likely would also include any done by himself. It matters little what the wrong done to or by Mr Redlaw actually was. It is the fact that a wrong was done and that memories of that fact are so destructive.

Dickens seems powerless to stop the illegitimate characters populating his novels, and in 1852 he starts work on *Bleak House*. After one of the best opening scenes in all his novels, describing the mists enveloping everything around him, Dickens introduces Esther Summerson, aged about 12–13 years old. Note that in 1852 Ellen was also about 12 to 13 years old. At this early stage in the history, there is little indication of Esther's parentage, but from the following extract, it is pretty clear that she is illegitimate:

> Dinner was over, and my godmother and I were sitting at the table before the fire. The clock ticked, the fire clicked; not another sound had been heard in the room or in the house for I don't know how long. I happened to look timidly up from my stitching, across the table at my godmother, and I saw in her face, looking gloomily at me, 'It would have been far better, little Esther, that you had had no birthday, that you had never been born!'
>
> I broke out crying and sobbing, and I said, 'Oh, dear godmother, tell me, pray do tell me, did Mama die on my birthday?'

'No,' she returned. 'Ask me no more, child!'

'Oh, do pray tell me something of her. Do now, at last, dear godmother, if you please! What did I do to her? How did I lose her? Why am I so different from other children, and why is it my fault, dear godmother? No, no, no, don't go away. Oh, speak to me!' I was in a kind of fright beyond my grief, and I caught hold of her dress and was kneeling to her. She had been saying all the while, 'Let me go!' But now she stood still. Her darkened face had such power over me that it stopped me in the midst of my vehemence. I put up my trembling little hand to clasp hers or to beg her pardon with what earnestness I might, but withdrew it as she looked at me, and laid it on my fluttering heart. She raised me, sat in her chair, and standing me before her, said slowly in a cold, low voice – I see her knitted brow and pointed finger – 'Your mother, Esther, is your disgrace, and you were hers. The time will come – and soon enough – when you will understand this better and will feel it too, as no one save a woman can. I have forgiven her' – but her face did not relent – 'the wrong she did to me, and I say no more of it, though it was greater than you will ever know – than any one will ever know but I, the sufferer. For yourself, unfortunate girl, orphaned and degraded from the first of these evil anniversaries, pray daily that the sins of others be not visited upon your head, according to what is written. Forget your mother and leave all other people to forget her who will do her unhappy child that greatest kindness. Now, go!'

She checked me, however, as I was about to depart from her – so frozen as I was! – and added this, 'Submission, self-denial, diligent work, are the preparations for a life begun with such a shadow on it. You are different from other children, Esther, because you were not born, like them, in common sinfulness and wrath. You are set apart.

As the novel progresses, we learn that Esther's mother is now Lady Dedlock, but at the time of Esther's birth, she was plain Miss Honoraria Barbary, sister of the 'godmother' who had agreed to raise the child. One might be sympathetic toward Miss Barbary's somewhat unforgiving attitude toward Esther if she had, indeed, sacrificed her own happiness in order to care for and raise her sister's illegitimate child. I suppose it is possible that the vehement statement: 'I have forgiven the wrong she did to me, and I say no more of it, though it was greater than you will ever know – than any one will ever know but I, the sufferer', is also a statement of her own unrequited love for Esther's father.

It is later still that we are told that Esther's father was Captain Hawdon, originally a serving officer in the military, but at the time of his introduction into the novel, the mysterious Mr Nemo, the lowly copying clerk in a legal office who dies a lonely death and is buried in the dreary burying ground. It is worth remembering here, that Charles Dickens had worked as a clerk in a legal office, and that is the similarity between the relationships in *Bleak House* and in Dickens's and Ellen's lives.

The relationship between Esther and John Jarndyce has little to do with that between Ellen and Dickens, but has very much to do with the play *Uncle John* by J.B. Buckstone. In that play, Uncle John, a wealthy confirmed bachelor, had for many years supported and assisted the widow and daughter Eliza of his late friend, Mr Comfort. Right out of the blue, Uncle John decided it was time that he married, and accordingly proposed to the now 18-year-old Eliza, who accepted more out of duty than of love. This shocked his niece, his only living relative, who could see her inheritance slipping away, so she makes mischief by letting Uncle John know of Eliza's fondness for her art teacher, Mr Easel. John immediately withdraws his offer of marriage (to the initial satisfaction of the niece), so that Eliza is free to marry Mr Easel. However, the niece's hopes are dashed again when Uncle John marries Eliza's mother, Mrs Comfort. Thus, Eliza becomes Uncle John's daughter, and will eventually inherit his wealth.

In *Bleak House,* John Jarndyce recruits the young Esther as a companion to his ward Ada. As time passes, a nice relationship does develop between Jarndyce and Esther, and he does, like Uncle John, propose marriage. Esther, like Eliza, accepts out of duty. However, it becomes clear to Jarndyce that Esther's heart is already given over to Dr Woodcourt, so he withdraws his offer just as Uncle John did in order that Esther can be free to marry her lover.

It is no coincidence that five years later, Ellen played the part of Eliza to Dickens's Uncle John when Buckstone's play was performed as the 'After Play' to *The Frozen Deep* at Manchester. But more of that in due course.

1855 to 1857 sees Dickens embarked on *Little Dorrit.* This novel begins with Arthur Clennam returning to London 'from the East', where he has been working with his father, who had recently died. Arthur has brought with him his late father's watch which had been engraved with the mantra 'Do Not Forget', the significance of which he does not fully understand. However, he is convinced it relates to some previous wrongdoing that must be righted. Quite clearly this is an echo of the *Haunted Man*'s mantra 'Keep my Memory Green'. Arthur is determined to find the victim of the wrong, and if at all possible, to make reparation for it. When he meets Little Amy Dorrit at his mother's house, he is convinced that in some way this girl is involved. This conviction increases even more as he learns about her birth in the Marshalsea debtor's prison where her father has been incarcerated for so long he is affectionately referred to as 'The Father of The Marshalsea'. Amy's mother had died at her birth, and she has two elder siblings, both very self-centred, and who, like their father, see Amy as their skivvy. The self-sacrificing Amy takes all of this in her stride and uncomplainingly meets all their selfish needs.

It eventually transpires that the original wrong had been committed by Arthur's father, who prior to his marriage had fathered a child with a music-hall dancer. This wrong was then compounded by Arthur's great-uncle, who insisted that Arthur's father marry an extremely religious woman and that the young mother would hand over her baby, Arthur, to the newly wedded Mrs Clennam, who would then raise Arthur as her own child. The great-uncle later relented and added a codicil to his will leaving the dancer £1,000, or, if she predeceased the uncle, the £1,000 would pass to the youngest niece of the clarinet-playing dancing teacher, Mr Frederick Dorrit, who was the only person who stood friend for the young dancer. In other words, the £1,000 would have passed to Amy Dorrit, and would have secured the release of the family very much earlier than was the case. But Mrs Clennam had discovered the codicil attached to the will, and had removed it, thereby denying Arthur's birth mother her rightful inheritance resulting in her dying alone and in poverty, and keeping Amy Dorrit's family in prison much longer than was necessary. Thus the initial wrong was compounded multiple times by the religiously fanatical Mrs Clennam in order to punish Mr Clennam, the dancer, and Arthur for their sins. They were the wrongs that were included in the mantra 'Do not Forget'.

It seems clear that Dickens was, from the 'days you remember when Mary was born' (1838), haunted by his memories of a wrong-doing, and those memories became more vivid and disturbing as time progressed. Just as the disaster of 1858 was happening, that is what Dickens had seen coming since 1838, when Mary was born. Ellen was now making her entrance onto Dickens's worldly stage, but it was in a much more devastating and disrupting way than he had ever imagined.

Realising that very soon Ellen would somehow make her grand entrance, Dickens knew he would have to deal with it and further, make reparation for the eighteen years of neglect of Ellen and of her mother.

Chapter Three

Growing Apart

'There can be no disparity in marriage like unsuitability of mind and purpose.'

Mrs Strong; *David Copperfield*

In Chapter One I mentioned a letter that Dickens sent to Catherine shortly after they had become engaged. In it Dickens wrote of Catherine's sudden and uncalled for coldness, and for the need for her to mend her ways. To me, that letter – so reminiscent of the one he sent to Maria Beadnell when that romance ended, also mentioned in Chapter One – seems not to augur well for their future together.

In 1840, about four years after Dickens and Catherine married, the young Queen Victoria married her Prince Albert, and of course there was much happiness and jubilation in England as the great event was celebrated. Dickens and some of his friends joined in the fun with the exchange of several letters. Because Dickens was in the habit of destroying letters he had received, only those that he sent to others are available. In those letters he wrote of having fallen in love with the Queen, and of having dismal thoughts of running away. These letters are generally regarded as being high-spirited jokes, of being caught up with romantic ideas in the fun of the impending royal wedding. And maybe it was all a joke at the time. However, in other letters in the so-called joke, Dickens makes some rather spiteful remarks, including how Catherine aggravates him; how he loathes his parents, and detests his house. He writes of his wretchedness, of how his wife makes him miserable, and similar remarks of his children.

As I said, maybe this was all a 'joke' at the time as generally accepted, but knowing what became of his marriage eventually, and how the sentiments expressed within these 'joke' letters are mirrored in the letter quoted below, maybe there is just a hint of the old adage that 'many a true word is spoken in jest'.

In Chapter Two I included a short extract from a letter written by Dickens to Forster on or about 3 September 1857, in which he claimed that as far back as when Mary was born he had foreseen what was now befalling him. Here is the full letter, as it appears in Forster's *Life of Dickens,* first published in 1872, but copied here from the 1911 edition:

> Your letter of yesterday was so kind and hearty, and sounded so gently the many chords we have touched together, that I cannot leave it unanswered, though I have not much (to any purpose) to say. My reference to 'confidences' was merely to the relief of saying a word of what has long been pent up in my mind. Poor Catherine and I are not made for each other, and there is no help for it. It is not only that she makes me uneasy and unhappy, but that I make her so too – and much more so. She is exactly what you know, in the way of being amiable and complying; but we are strangely ill-assorted for the bond there is between us. God knows she would have been a thousand times happier if she had

married another kind of man, and that her avoidance of this destiny would have been at least equally good for us both. I am often cut to the heart by thinking what a pity it is, for her own sake, that I ever fell in her way; and if I were sick or disabled to-morrow, I know how sorry she would be, and how deeply grieved myself, to think how we had lost each other. But exactly the same incompatibility would arise, the moment I was well again; and nothing on earth could make her understand me, or suit us to each other. Her temperament will not go with mine. It mattered not so much when we had only ourselves to consider, but reasons have been growing since which make it all but hopeless that we should even try to struggle on. What is now befalling me I have seen steadily coming, ever since the days you remember when Mary was born; and I know too well that you cannot, and no one can, help me. Why I have even written I hardly know; but it is a miserable sort of comfort that you should be clearly aware how matters stand. The mere mention of the fact, without any complaint or blame of any sort, is a relief to my present state of spirits – and I can get this only from you, because I can speak of it to no one else.' In the same tone was his rejoinder to my reply. 'To the most part of what you say – Amen! You are not so tolerant as perhaps you might be of the wayward and unsettled feeling which is part (I suppose) of the tenure on which one holds an imaginative life, and which I have, as you ought to know well, often only kept down by riding over it like a dragoon – but let that go by. I make no maudlin complaint. I agree with you as to the very possible incidents, even not less bearable than mine, that might and must often occur to the married condition when it is entered into very young. I am always deeply sensible of the wonderful exercise I have of life and its highest sensations, and have said to myself for years, and have honestly and truly felt, this is the drawback to such a career, and is not to be complained of. I say it and feel it now as strongly as ever I did; and, as I told you in my last, I do not with that view put all this forward. But the years have not made it easier to bear for either of us; and, for her sake as well as mine, the wish will force itself upon me that something might be done. I know too well it is impossible. There is the fact, and that is all one can say. Nor are you to suppose that I disguise from myself what might be urged on the other side. I claim no immunity from blame. There is plenty of fault on my side, I dare say, in the way of a thousand uncertainties, caprices, and difficulties of disposition; but only one thing will alter all that, and that is, the end which alters everything.

About the deteriorating state of his marriage, I need say no more. We know that shortly after all this Dickens and Catherine did separate, and that this would probably happen was clear for some time, perhaps from the 'Joke' letters following the marriage of Queen Victoria in 1840, and certainly from the writing of *Copperfield*.

Let us now look at a point roughly half-way through his marriage, 1849–50 when he was writing *David Copperfield*.

Copperfield is largely seen as being autobiographical, and we can certainly see the obviously biographical details such as the blacking factory, the debtor's prison, the legal office and his becoming an author. But is it fair to think that David's marriage to Dora is also biographical, and a reflection of Dickens's marriage to Catherine? Before I try to answer that, I want to look very briefly at David's first visit to the theatre with Steerforth and other friends which is described in Book VIII, written in November 1849. They first have a dinner at David's apartment, and David certainly drinks more than was good for him. As a result, he rather embarrassed himself at the theatre and the play does not actually get a mention, so we cannot be sure what it was. However, the following day he was invited to a lunch with a friend of Mr Wickfield and several other guests. Agnes was there, but David was disappointed at finding himself not sitting next to Agnes, instead sitting next to 'a relative of Hamlet, perhaps his aunt'. Is there any reason why, of all the characters, Shakespearean or otherwise, Dickens could have sat at that table, he nominated Hamlet's aunt? Is it perhaps because he was thinking of Mrs Ternan, who, having played Ophelia many times in her younger days, was now being seen on the stage more often playing Hamlet's mother Gertrude. Following Mr Ternan's death, Mrs Ternan and the three girls largely toured England and Ireland, performing with very good reviews in the provincial theatres. This continued until the end of December 1849, at which time Mrs Ternan was engaged by Mr James Anderson, the new lessee of the Theatre Royal, Drury Lane, for the 1850 season. There were notices advertising this engagement in many London newspapers and periodicals through the latter part of 1849, so it is most likely that Dickens was aware of her impending reappearance on the London stage. Just before leaving the provinces, she was playing Gertrude, and would play that role again in April 1850. And as we know, Hamlet's mother Gertrude becomes his aunt when she marries the brother of his murdered father. Maybe that is the play and the character that Dickens had in his mind when David went to the theatre, and why David found himself sitting next to Hamlet's aunt the following day.

But back to David and Dora. Here is an extract of another letter Dickens wrote to Forster (in February 1855), just five years after writing *Copperfield*. (Again, from Forster, *Life of Dickens*.) 'Am altogether in a dishevelled state of mind ... Why is it, that as with poor David, a sense comes always crushing on me now, when I fall into low spirits, as of one happiness I have missed in life, and one friend and companion I have never made?'

So if one bears those letters in mind while reading the following half-dozen extracts from *David Copperfield* in which David is musing on his marriage to Dora, one could very well imagine Dickens having the same thoughts about his own marriage to Catherine.

> It seemed such an extraordinary thing to have Dora always there. It was so unaccountable not to be obliged to go out to see her, not to have any occasion to be tormenting myself about her, not to have to write to her, not to be scheming and devising opportunities of being alone with her. Sometimes of an evening, when I looked up from my writing and saw her seated opposite, I would lean back in my chair, and think how

queer it was that there we were, alone together as a matter of course – nobody's business any more – all the romance of our engagement put away upon a shelf, to rust – no one to please but one another to please, for life.

When there was a debate, and I was kept out very late, it seemed so strange to me, as I was walking home, to think that Dora was at home! It was such a wonderful thing, at first, to have her coming softly down to talk to me as I ate my supper…

The old unhappy feeling pervaded my life. It was deepened, if it were changed at all; but it was as undefined as ever, and addressed me like a strain of sorrowful music faintly heard in the night. I loved my wife dearly, and I was happy; but the happiness I had vaguely anticipated, once, was not the happiness I enjoyed, and there was always something wanting.

The old unhappy loss or want of something had, I am conscious, some place in my heart; but not to the embitterment of my life. When I walked alone in the fine weather, and thought of the summer days when all the air had been filled with my boyish enchantment, I did miss something of the realisation of my dreams; but I thought it was a softened glory of the Past, which nothing could have thrown upon the present time. I did feel, sometimes, for a little while, that I could have wished my wife had been my counsellor; had

had more character and purpose, to sustain me and to improve me by; had been endowed with power to fill up the void which somewhere seemed to be about me; but I felt as if it were an unearthly consummation of my happiness, that never had been meant to be, and never could have been.

But that it would have been better for me if my wife could have helped me more, and shared the many thoughts in which I had no partner; and that this might have been; I knew.

Sometimes, the speculations came into my thoughts, What might have happened, or what would have happened, if Dora and I had never known each other?

'There can be no disparity in marriage like unsuitability of mind and purpose.' Those words I remembered too. I had endeavoured to adapt Dora to myself, and found it impracticable. It remained for me to adapt myself to Dora; to share with her what I could, and be happy; to bear on my own shoulders that I must, and be happy still.

These musings of David refer to the first couple of years of their marriage. We might apply them to that equivalent period of Dickens's marriage to Catherine, which in terms of time, would bring it close to the 'days you remember when Mary was born'. But equally, it could have been Dickens reflecting on the state of his marriage at the time of his actually writing *Copperfield,* by which time Ellen was about 11 years old, and growing up. An illegitimate child known to be there by the father, and maybe suspected by his wife, would not have made for a harmonious life. And then in April 1856, when Ellen is a blooming 17-year-old, Dickens writes to Forster having just learned of Macready's retirement. The letter starts with Dickens reflecting on Macready's retirement, then reflecting on how he will not get to retire. First, he would rather die in harness, and second, he knows full well the demands on his purse are so great he cannot afford to retire. He then thinks of his past: (Forster, *Life of Dickens*):

> The old days – The old days! Shall I ever, I wonder, get the frame of mind back as it used to be then? Something of it perhaps – but never quite the same as it used to be. I find that the skeleton in my domestic closet is becoming a pretty big one.

'The old days, the old days.' Is it drawing too long a bow to think that here Dickens is once again reminding Forster of 'Those days you remember when Mary was born'? He has managed thus far to conceal Ellen from everyone, but as she is now nearly an adult and is out there on the professional stage, there are very real possibilities that what he has seen coming since those days is about to appear. The idiomatic expression 'skeleton in the closet' has always been used to signify a source of something scandalous or shameful. It is generally used when referring to something in the past that will cause potential ruin to a person when exposed, or at least damage his or her reputation and social standing in the community were it to be revealed. This letter was intended exclusively for the eyes of his most trusted friend, John Forster; Dickens never envisaged that it would find its way into the public domain. Why would he use the expression in any way other than its generally accepted meaning? I think it is also important to note the use of the possessive 'my' in relation to the skeleton. It is not the family closet, not a family secret, but that of Dickens alone. And if it is not referring to Ellen, who or what else could the skeleton be, coming as it did from the old days when Mary was born?

It has been suggested that in the 'skeleton is becoming a pretty big one', Dickens is referring to Catherine's increased weight. However, I think it unlikely that Dickens would have seen Catherine's weight increasing as far back as 1838 when Mary was born, in the 'old days'. Maybe Dickens was disappointed by the change in Catherine's body, but I believe that those two letters to Forster, especially the statements of 'what is befalling me now' and the 'skeleton in my closet', are probably the most telling of all the letters. Forster saw a lot of the Dickens family, and would have been well aware of Catherine's build and what Dickens might, or might not have thought about it. Dickens was not writing to strangers or to someone he had not seen for a decade or two, explaining how Catherine was at this time – he was writing exclusively to Forster. In that context, it would have been unnecessary for Dickens to use the analogy of a skeleton in the cupboard to describe Catherine if he were writing to Forster. I have no doubt that within the context of those letters at this time, Dickens was definitely referring to an event in the past (not the present), the outcome of which was to haunt him for nearly twenty years as the skeleton grew, just as Ellen did.

Of course, we do not have the letters that Forster might have written to Dickens in response to the 'skeleton' letter, nor to the 'what is befalling me now' letter, but it is interesting to note how Forster dealt with these letters in his *Life of Dickens*. He makes no reference at all to the skeleton, not even hinting at what it might have meant. He also makes no mention of what he is being encouraged to remember about the time when Mary was born. My belief is that they are both really tied up with Ellen, and that Forster consciously made no public comment in his *Life* for the same reason that he left Ellen out of the whole biography. However, neither of these two letters have been particularly stressed in most biographies I have read, for no reason, I suspect, other than that they predate *The Frozen Deep*.

I believe that Dickens was becoming increasingly conscious of the possibility of the skeleton reappearing, and if that was to be the case, he would make sure it happened in a way that he could control.

An opportunity to manage her grand entrance was about to appear.

Chapter Four

Plans for Making Reparation

The best laid schemes o' Mice an' Men Gang aft agley,
To a Mouse by Robert Burns

That opportunity to make reparation was to present itself with the demise, on 8 June 1857, of Dickens's good friend, the dramatist Douglas Jerrold. Following the great success of *The Frozen Deep* performed by the Dickens Amateurs to invited audiences in the makeshift 'theatre' in the children's nursery at Tavistock House, Dickens and the rest of the cast decided to perform the play to paying audiences to raise funds for Jerrold's widow and unmarried daughter. They initially relocated to the nearby Gallery of Illustration, but while this could accommodate a few more people, including Queen Victoria (who thoroughly enjoyed the play, but was probably admitted without charge!), it still did not hold enough to raise very much in the way of funds. Thus, they decided to hire the huge Free Trades Hall in Manchester, large enough to accommodate over 2,500 people, which would raise a considerable sum but which would also necessitate the recruitment of some professional female actors. One mature and two younger players would be needed to take those parts previously acted by Georgina, Mary and Katey, whose untrained voices would not carry across such a huge venue.

In the relict of Douglas Jerrold, Dickens would have seen a reflection of the widowed Mrs Ternan and her three daughters. With no widow's pensions or any other social security payments such as we have today, a widow, especially one with young children, would struggle to keep a roof over the family's heads. Even before she was widowed, Mrs Ternan had been the main breadwinner, and would probably have learned the tricks of making a little go a long way, but I doubt that she would have had very much in the way of savings to fall back on. Dickens, already troubled by his conscience, might have even contemplated the possibility of Ellen ending up at Urania Cottage (the Home for Homeless Women) should Mrs Ternan be incapacitated in any way.

I have a hunch that Dickens saw an opportunity to finally come face to face with his skeleton in the cupboard, by recruiting Mrs Ternan and her daughters to the cast of *The Frozen Deep*. Given his reputation, Dickens would have had no difficulty in recruiting actors from anywhere; instead, he asked his friend, theatre manager Alfred Wigan – knowing that the Ternan ladies were established as part of his stable – to approach Mrs Ternan to determine whether they would be interested in the job. By doing so, he would create the opportunity to recruit the whole family at 'arms-length' without having to approach them himself. If nothing else came of it, at least it would have had the financial advantage that the Ternans, being a family, could readily share the same lodgings at Manchester, thereby reducing the costs. But the underlying reasons for specifically recruiting the Ternans was to finally establish whether the memory that had been haunting him since June 1838, that he might have been Ellen's father, was real or imagined. If it turned out to be the case that Ellen was his child, he would then have the advantage, right from the start, of being in control.

I think it is pertinent here to mention a 1928 'biography' of Dickens by one Carl Eric Bechhofer Roberts, published by Mills and Boon, and with the title *This Side Idolatry*. I enclosed the word 'biography' in inverted commas because while Roberts had initially wished to write a standard biography, difficulties with the Dickens family regarding permission to quote from hitherto unpublished letters to Maria Beadnell left him with no alternative other than to put the words into the mouth of a fictionalised Dickens, and publish as a novel. It largely follows the information found in Forster's *Life of Charles Dickens*, but of course there are also fictional elements. Much of the book – the aim of which appears to be toppling Dickens off the pedestal upon which Roberts thinks he has been unjustifiably placed – is irrelevant to the relationship between Dickens and Ellen Ternan. It deals more with family relationships, his treatment of his parents and of Catherine, and with Maria Winter, née Beadnell. Although Ellen does get an oblique reference in relation to the separation of Dickens and Catherine, there is no actual statement about the role she might or might not have played. But what I think is more relevant is an anecdote which no one can be actually sure is part of the fiction or part of the truth. While most authors who have commented on it do admit its veracity is unclear, they generally make a comment about it just in case it is a truth! For my part, I am happy to believe that it does have at least a grain of truth in it.

The anecdote comes toward the end of the book, and tells of Dickens going backstage at the Haymarket theatre and finding Ellen there, embarrassed and distressed at the scanty costume she has been required to wear as the character Prince Hippomenes in a burlesque production of the classical myth *Atalanta*. Roberts gives no reference to his source of the anecdote (perhaps simply observing the journalist's policy of not disclosing the source of his information), but in June 1857 Ellen was definitely acting that part in that play at that theatre. June 1857, of course, was when Dickens was casting for *The Frozen Deep*, and more importantly for *Uncle John*, and I believe it very likely that he would have attended at least one performance by Ellen, even if for no reason other than to check the quality of her acting.

The other point I will make about *This Side Idolatry* is that it's more about what Roberts did *not* say about Ellen than what he did. Roberts was a professional journalist, and it seems that his main reason for writing the book was to show that Dickens was not the upright citizen with a strong moral compass, nor the perfect husband and family man of the domestic hearth, as portrayed in the varnished portraits hitherto painted. Since Roberts was so keen to topple Dickens from his pedestal, surely, as a journalist digging for dirt, had he sniffed out so much as a whiff of a sexual relationship between Dickens and Ellen he would have made much, much more of it. But writing as he was in the mid-1920s, some seven to nine years prior to the publication of Thomas Wright's and Gladys Storey's claims, he was completely untainted by them, and therefore wrote only what he could discover for himself, and what he did discover clearly did not include Ellen possibly being the mistress of Dickens.

To return to the casting for *The Frozen Deep* – and here I fully admit that this is pure speculation. Dickens specifically recruited the Ternan family so that he could orchestrate and control Ellen's entry into his world, and we must not lose sight of the fact that there was also the casting for the after-play, *Uncle John*. While nearly all biographers of Charles Dickens refer to *The Frozen Deep* in great detail, they mostly pay scant attention to *Uncle John*. To borrow an expression used by Michael Slater in his wonderful book *The Great Charles Dickens Scandal*,[28] I think that by doing so, they have all missed a trick! *Uncle John*, as we have seen earlier (see Chapter Two on *Bleak House*), tells of a widow, Mrs Comfort, and her daughter Eliza, being financially assisted for about eighteen years by Uncle John, who, by a quirk at the end of the play, makes Eliza his daughter by marrying her mother. In recruiting the Ternans for Manchester, Dickens then casts Mrs Ternan as Mrs Comfort, and Ellen as Eliza. For eighteen years Uncle John had watched Eliza grow up. For eighteen years Dickens could only *imagine* how Ellen was progressing. Now here was a chance for him to enact those eighteen years alongside Mrs Ternan and Ellen, and see if he could really establish once and for all whether Ellen was, or was not, his daughter. If he was able to confirm it, he would then be able to make provision for her and for the widowed Mrs Ternan, in an obvious and outwardly platonic way, much as Buckstone's *Uncle John* had provided for Eliza and her widowed mother. Like the widow and daughter of Douglas Jerrold, the Ternans would have simply become part of his circle of theatrical friends, and he could have slowly increased his support for them, in the way of accommodation etc.

So far, the plan was working. The performances were a huge success, both theatrically and financially. Dickens himself, stimulated by finally being able to spend time with his daughter, gave the performances of his life. Many biographers have commented on the way Dickens responded with great excitement and enthusiasm when he was contacted by his adolescent love, Maria Beadnell, now the middle-aged Mrs Winter. They have also commented on how shattered he was when he met her and found her very much changed. It is not unlikely that his determination to contact Mrs Ternan for the Manchester performances was perhaps coloured with some trepidation as to what might happen. But all went swimmingly, and he would have been as elated with this reunion with Mrs Ternan as he was disappointed with his meeting with Mrs Winter. The flame that had existed in June 1838 burned bright again, fanned by being on the stage working his way through *Uncle John* with Mrs Ternan and his daughter Ellen. And it was the glow from that rekindled flame and the spring in his step that led to the assumption by many commentators that he was obsessed with, and en route to seducing, Ellen.

Following the short season, everybody was jubilant as they all went first to London and then their separate ways, which for the Ternans was to Doncaster where they had another engagement. Dickens, elated with the success of his plans and very keen to find out more about his daughter, found an excuse to travel to Doncaster for the St Leger Day Races, along with his very good friend and fellow co-star in *The Frozen Deep*, Wilkie Collins. This was ostensibly to gather material for a short series of sketches,

The Lazy Tour of Two Idle Apprentices, but is considered by most biographers to be an excuse to visit the Ternans at Doncaster. It seems that Dickens was not quite sure about how long he would stay at Doncaster, and after attending the races with the Ternans, he suddenly left to return to London. This apparent retreat has, of course, been interpreted – wrongly, I think – as Dickens 'pursuing' Ellen (with a view to seduction) but perhaps being 'warned off' by Mrs Ternan.

At this time, Dickens did write to his trusted assistant William Henry Wills[29] (always referred to simply as Wills) saying, inter alia, that he was at Doncaster because of Richard Wardour, and challenging Wills to solve the riddle. A few days later he wrote again to Wills,[30] telling him that he is going to take the 'little riddle' into the country that morning. He goes on to indicate that he might leave Doncaster on Tuesday, but could not be sure, and ends the letter with 'so let the riddle and the riddler go their own wild way'.

Claire Tomalin interprets this as Dickens telling Wills that he is in pursuit of Ellen, and hopeful enough of success to be postponing his return south. However, I think Tomalin has misunderstood the situation, and has misinterpreted the letter to Wills. The relationship between a 'riddler' and the 'riddle' is simply that the one gives rise to the other. Thus, rather than spell it out completely, this is Dickens telling Wills in a jocular way that Ellen is his daughter, not his quarry. He must tell *someone* – after all he has kept this bottled up for eighteen years – and in this jesting way is able to confide in his trusted friend, Wills. Like his letters to Forster, these letters to Wills were never meant for public consumption and Dickens would have considered his secret to be safe.

Claire Tomalin then suggests that either something in Ellen's own behaviour, or perhaps a warning from her mother, made Dickens draw back from his headlong wooing. 'Headlong wooing' might be one explanation of Dickens's behaviour at this stage. More likely I think, is that the uncommon interest he was showing in Ellen was merely to the point of discovering more about her, to see if he could finally burst the ever-intrusive thought bubble in his head, and answer the question, 'is she my daughter?' I believe that he did find that answer, possibly told to him by Mrs Ternan as part of the 'warning from her mother'.

But before we leave Doncaster, let us look at *The Lazy Tour of Two Idle Apprentices*, the gathering of copy for which the trip to Doncaster was made in the first place. What was eventually published as part of the *Tour* was: 'O little lilac gloves! And O winning little bonnet, making in conjunction with her golden hair quite a Glory in the sunlight round the pretty head, why anything in the world but you and me!'

And this has been interpreted as a strong sign of Dickens's infatuation with Ellen. But before we get too carried away with that interpretation, read this next extract: 'O look at her little ribbons, frills, and edges, at her shawl, at her gloves, at her hair, at her bracelets, at her bonnet, at everything about her!'

These two extracts seem to me to be strikingly similar, so are they both about Ellen? Maybe, maybe not. The second of these two extracts comes from *A Flight*, referred to earlier, which was written and published in 1851, and refers to the Compact Enchantress sitting opposite the traveller (presumably Dickens himself) on the train from London to Paris. She is in the company of 'Mystery', and is nursing a pineapple in her lap. It is also important to note that *A*

Flight, while first published in 1851 (when Ellen was only 12 years old and the Enchantress judged to be an unknown French actress at the St James's Theatre) was later included in *Reprinted Pieces* in 1858, which would have been in the publishing pipeline in 1857. It is very likely, therefore, that the description of the gloves, bonnet, hair etc was already at the forefront of Dickens's mind even before the Doncaster Races, and therefore not at all an indicator of Dickens's state of mind following *The Frozen Deep*. And certainly not part of his pursuance of Ellen as a potential mistress. As an aside, it is interesting to note that in 1865 Dickens was travelling in a train with Ellen (a Compact Enchantress?) and a mystery woman (presumably Mrs Ternan!).

And having now established as a certainty what had been for so long just a suspicion, Dickens was suddenly confronted with the next question 'What do I do now?' He knew he now had to make reparation for those eighteen years of neglect, so he immediately returned to London to clear his head and to start that process. So far, still so good. His plan for making reparation was all falling nicely into place.

But what he did not foresee, what he could not have foreseen, and therefore what he was powerless to control, was the sudden accusation, by his mother-in-law, of his having an affair with his sister-in-law Georgina!

Once the accusations of an affair with Georgina began to circulate, Dickens was, to say the least, between a rock and a hard place. Clearly, he could not just sit back and let it go; accusations of incest (as the connection between a husband and his wife's sister was legally defined at the time) would have ruined him. He might have got away with accusations of having a mistress, but not incest. He resorted to the most radical solution, and that was to require Georgina to be examined by a doctor. Fortunately for him, Georgina, who by association was also in the firing line of the accusers, agreed to the examination, as much for her own sake as for that of Dickens, I would think. Happily, it was proved beyond doubt that Georgina was indeed *virgo intacta*, and thus those particular accusations were proven to be false – although it did not put a stop to them entirely, and one gutter reporter went as far as claiming that three of Dickens's children had been born to Georgina rather than Catherine.

While at his club one day William Thackeray heard of the Georgina accusation. In a letter to his mother he said: 'No such thing, said I. It was with an actress.'

Whether he was just trying to be helpful is unclear, but while he did not name any actress, it wasn't long before Ellen's name was attached in the place of Georgina's. This did not help Dickens at all. He was still furious and wrote what became known as his 'Personal Statement' and also his 'Violated Letter'. In the Personal Statement he wrote, inter alia, 'of misrepresentations, most monstrous, and most cruel involving … innocent persons dear to my heart'. Then, in the 'Violated Letter' he wrote – again not mentioning any names (but most probably Catherine's mother and sister Helen) – that 'two wicked persons … have coupled with this separation the name of a young lady … (whom) I know to be as pure as my own dear daughters'. As I have stated, no names were mentioned in either the Statement or the Letter, but the use in the Statement of the plural 'innocent persons' indicates at least two, the most likely candidates being, of course, Georgina and Ellen. And of the 'young lady' mentioned in the Letter, it almost certainly was the 18-year-old Ellen, rather than the 30-year-old Georgina. But if he had seduced, or was working toward the seduction of, Ellen, is it likely that he (or any other man in that situation) would then compare the morals of his mistress with those of his unmarried daughters? I would think not! But to compare the morals of an illegitimate daughter with his other, legitimate, daughters would be completely in order.

He could not admit to having a mistress, or to fathering an illegitimate child. Either way, it would have been an admission of his infidelity to Catherine, whenever it might have happened and whoever it was with. It would also have tarnished the reputations of Mrs Ternan, branded an adulteress, as she would have been, and of Ellen, who would have carried the stigma of illegitimacy which could have damaged her marriage prospects, among other consequences. Fortunately, illegitimacy is not a problem today, but when Ellen was living in the nineteenth century, an illegitimate child was deemed, legally, to be *filius nullius* – literally, 'no one's child'. Attitudes slowly changed, and there were small reforms improving the legal rights of children born to unmarried parents from 1926 onwards, and as recently as 1987 the legal distinction between legitimate and illegitimate was finally eradicated from English statutes.

This turn of events took Dickens completely by surprise, and in his anger, his devastation at his plans being frustrated, he did what any cut snake would do, and that was to lose control of his emotions and lash out at those around him. It has often been wondered why he acted as he did, writing the 'Personal Statement' and the 'Violated Letter', which only compounded the problems he was to face. I suspect it was a moment of insanity brought on by the already existing stresses of trying to introduce Ellen quietly into his world, and the gross interference from his wife's mother and the youngest of Catherine's sisters, Helen. The unjust and malicious accusations of a sexual relationship with his sister-in-law were simply far too much to bear, and could not be ignored. Having lashed out as he did, he could no longer even try to maintain the appearance of a platonic relationship with Mrs Ternan and Ellen. It is no wonder that his daughter Katey later described him as being a mad man at that time.

Dickens scholars would be fully aware of both the 'Violated Letter' and the 'Personal Statement', but for those not familiar with them, they are available in both the Nonesuch edition and the Pilgrim edition of *The Letters of Charles Dickens*. They are also included as appendices in Slater's *Great Charles Dickens Scandal*.

After these letters had been circulated, Dickens was, to put it mildly, annoyed at their widespread distribution – despite the fact that he had expressly requested that they be brought to the attention of anyone! They were clearly written when he was extremely angry, and he could not, surely, do other than regret his actions. However, Dickens's pride was now satisfied. He had given the detractors a public dressing down, and having got through the distractions, could now get on with his day jobs. These were still, of course, publishing *Household Words*, writing novels, and giving readings. But he still needed to continue with his plans to make reparation to Ellen and to her mother for those eighteen years of neglect. But now, particularly after Ellen's name had been substituted for Georgina's in the scurrilous accusations, he had no option other than to do it clandestinely. And that is what he did. With no paparazzi, with no social media at the time, he was able to hide Ellen away while providing for her. But before we move on, this might be an appropriate place to speculate on why Mrs Hogarth did make such damaging statements about Dickens and Georgina.

In 1854, Dickens wrote *Hard Times*, which I believe is the only one of his novels to include a character seriously contemplating a divorce. Stephen Blackpool, a mill worker, is in a very unsatisfactory marriage with a seriously mentally compromised and addicted woman. He seeks the advice of Mr Bounderby, who tells him in no uncertain terms that divorce would be impossible, and actually describes the process in some detail.

> 'Now, I tell you what!' said Mr Bounderby, putting his hands in his pockets. 'There is such a law … But it's not for you at all. It costs money. It costs a mint of money.'

> 'How much might that be?' Stephen calmly asked.

> 'Why, you'd have to go to Doctors' Commons with a suit, and you'd have to go to a court of Common Law with a suit, and you'd have to go to the House of Lords with a suit, and you'd have to get an Act of Parliament to enable you to marry again, and it would cost you (if it was a case of very plain sailing), I suppose from a thousand to fifteen hundred pound,' said Mr Bounderby. 'Perhaps twice the money.'

'There's no other law? Asked Stephen

'Certainly not!'

Dickens had obviously done his homework on divorce proceedings, and already knew, through his association with the case of his friend Bulwer Lytton, that divorce was only available to those with unlimited financial resources and with friends in high places. So one might wonder whether even in 1854 Dickens was contemplating a divorce? But it might also have had something to do with the fact that in 1854 the Matrimonial Causes Bill was just starting its tortuous route through the House of Commons. This bill, when enacted, would remove marriage and divorce from the Ecclesiastical Courts, where it was dealt with as a matter of sanctity, and place it squarely in the civil courts as a matter of contract law. This would have been very controversial at the time, with the Archbishop of Canterbury in favour of the change, whereas others in the hierarchy of the church were vehemently opposed. No doubt it would have been a major talking point at the time.

Apart from that major change to the process, the new bill also made it slightly easier for a man to divorce his wife, bringing the whole process within reach of the common man. The only grounds really needed were insanity of the wife, or her adultery. However, while it was previously almost impossible for the wife to secure a divorce, the Bill would also make it possible for the wife to be successful, if she had the grounds. The Bill was eventually passed into law in 1857, just as the Dickens's marriage was on the brink of collapse. So did

Catherine actually consider the possibility of her obtaining the divorce under the new Act? Maybe. But she needed the appropriate grounds to be successful, and Dickens's adultery (whether it was with Mrs Ternan in 1838 or Ellen in 1858) would not have been sufficient on its own. She would have needed additional grounds, one of which was the husband having an incestuous relationship, which, at the time, included adultery with one's sister-in-law. I raise it simply as a speculation, I certainly have no answer.

Chapter Five

Making Reparation, Plan B

If at first you don't succeed, try, try again.
                                   Possibly Robert the Bruce

So after the outbursts of righteous indignation described in the previous chapter, Dickens picked up his pen and started work on *A Tale of Two Cities*. Matters seemed to calm down a lot, and he got on with his work. The Ternans just seem to have vanished into thin air, apparently with a little help from Dickens.

The eldest daughter, Frances, was probably the best actor of the three, and certainly showed promise as a singer. An opportunity arose for her to go to Italy for singing lessons and to further her career, and it appears that Dickens funded the trip for her, and for her mother who was just on the cusp of retirement anyway, to accompany her as chaperone. Meanwhile, the two younger daughters stayed on in London, essentially under the guardianship of Dickens, both Maria and Ellen continuing on the stage at this time, that being their only means of support.

It is difficult to believe that Mrs Ternan, who had a reputation for high moral standards and who had brought up her daughters with those same standards, would have countenanced such an arrangement were she not absolutely convinced of the safety of her younger daughters. However, it has been suggested that she was even complicit in Dickens's desire to seduce Ellen. Under such circumstances, the risk of Ellen being debauched and then dumped as damaged goods would surely have been too high to take. But by leaving Maria and Ellen under the watchful eye of Ellen's father, Mrs Ternan would have been assured that her two younger daughters would indeed be safely looked after while she was away.

Meanwhile, in Italy, Frances was appointed as governess to Beatrice (Bice), the daughter of the widowed Thomas Adolphus (Tom) Trollope. In due course, Frances and Tom married, Frances established herself as a writer, and the marriage lasted until Tom's death in 1892. Frances was to die in 1913. Given Frances's independence through her marriage to Tom Trollope, and through her own abilities as a writer, Dickens's investment in her trip to Italy paid off, and she was never again a charge on his purse.

Mrs Ternan had returned to England well before her daughter's marriage to Tom Trollope, and it became very clear that she also left the theatre at that time, returning for a short season with Fetcher as 'blind Alice' in an 1866 production of *The Bride of Lammermoor*. Maria also left the acting profession and, following a not very successful marriage, went on to an independent life as a journalist and writer, travelling widely through Europe and parts of Africa. This left Mrs Ternan and Ellen as the only two Ternans dependent on Dickens. By June 1858, Charles and Catherine Dickens had separated, with Catherine moving out of Tavistock House to live nearby in accommodation provided by Dickens. The separation agreement provided Catherine with a house, some domestic staff, a carriage with horses and (presumably) a groom, and £600 per year, all funded by Dickens. Whether it was Dickens throwing her out, or Catherine asking for and being given her freedom remains uncertain and still a matter of speculation. In Dickens's 'Violated Letter' he had indicated that Catherine had indeed begged him to let her live separately, but Georgina had persuaded them against separation at that time.

Just as Catherine was set up in her own home at Dickens's expense, so Mrs Ternan and Ellen were also provided with accommodation and living expenses by Dickens. It appears that he might have considered their using Tavistock House, but was apparently advised by Forster not to take that route. Someone, presumably Dickens, purchased, in the names of 'Frances and Maria Ternan (spinsters)', a long-term lease on the nearby Houghton House in Ampthill. Ampthill, now a housing estate of multi-storey dwellings in the London Borough of Camden, was originally developed in 1800 as a garden estate by the Duke of Bedford, and is named after the town of Ampthill in Bedfordshire where the Duke had his country seat. The Houghton House purchased by Dickens was eponymous for the Duke's stately home at Ampthill, a rather grand pile, now in ruins. It would have been most unlikely that the two girls could have raised the sort of financial resources needed to have bought into such a prestigious address without some help, so the presumption that it was indeed Dickens who provided the money is most likely correct. He would have seen this as a sensible step he could take toward making Mrs Ternan, and Ellen in particular, independent, as a year later the two sisters 'sold' the lease to Ellen. Of this purchase Claire Tomalin opined that while it was a measure of Dickens's seriousness and a guarantee of Ellen's future security, it was a gift no 'respectable' woman would have accepted, and no mother who cherished her daughter's good name would have permitted. Of course, Tomalin is making those statements believing the standard Wright/Storey narrative, and assuming it was a way for Dickens to acquire Ellen like a male bowerbird attracting his mate with a very elaborate nest. Under those circumstances it certainly would not have been acceptable to a mother who cherishes her daughter's good name. But if one looks at it from the perspective of Ellen being his daughter rather than a potential mistress, it was not only an excellent way of securing her future, possibly keeping her out of Urania Cottage or similar establishments, it was also a very right and proper course for him to take. The lease was for eighty-four years, and would have ensured Ellen's security well past her 100th birthday, had she reached that milestone. As it happened, she finally sold the lease after holding it for thirty years.

The Dickenses' eldest son Charles moved in with his mother; the rest of their children who had not died or gone overseas stayed with Dickens. This of course included the two daughters, Mary – who remained with her father until his death in 1870 – and Katey, who left home in July 1860 to marry Charles Collins, the brother of Wilkie. Another way of looking at it is that Dickens set up his two families on roughly equal footings, just as Wilkie Collins had set up his two mistresses – the difference being that Wilkie had run his two households concurrently, whereas Dickens had set them up consecutively.

What does seem clear is that Mrs Ternan and Ellen lived very much as a widowed mother and her daughter might be expected to live. However, various biographers, including Harrison, have commented rather sarcastically that Dickens's shrewish, greedy little gold-digging mistress was always accompanied by her wide-awake mother. There was one report, seemingly originally told by a pianist friend of Dickens, that he remembered being with Dickens and the Ternans at this time, playing the piano while the others sang and enjoyed themselves. Harrison describes this as them all being in their grubby little love nest. I see it as a mother and father, occasionally together with their daughter, entertaining themselves just as any other nineteenth-century family would have done prior to television. However, it was by keeping the Ternans moving into a variety of different addresses, rented under a variety of assumed names such as Tringham, Turnan and Turnham that seemed to keep them very much out of the public scrutiny at the time (and there is doubt even as to the veracity of the anecdote).

From this point in time, Dickens returned to his day job and went about his business as usual, writing, attending various functions, participating in charitable events, and organising his reading tours in the UK and the US. Quite clearly his focus was now on maintaining, and hopefully even increasing, his income. He was supporting three separate households containing a total of twelve family members and an unknown number of domestic staff. There was also his ageing ailing mother, his sons – who seem to have inherited their paternal grandfather's profligacy genes and were constantly in debt – and several other struggling family members. He was also wishing to purchase Gad's Hill. In addition to these domestic drains on his purse there was the staff and other expenses of *Household Words*, and those associated with his reading tours.

His financial responsibilities were enormous and he could see no end to it. It is no wonder that when ruminating on Macready's retirement he added that for some, 'there is no such repose'. Eventually, as interest waned, all the rumours surrounding the separation of Catherine and Dickens seemed to die down as such things do. Meanwhile, Ellen and Mrs Ternan moved around, both locally and in France, sometimes staying with Frances or with Maria, the two married daughters. The rest of the time they would be living alone with the occasional visit by Dickens himself.

Dickens continued his writings, completing three more major novels, (*A Tale of Two Cities, Great Expectations, Our Mutual Friend*), and the unfinished *Mystery of Edwin Drood*. His reading tours both in America and at home were enormously successful, with every performance completely sold out. During this time he made several visits to France; he had always loved going since his very first trip. His French language skills were more than just passable, and at one stage he even described himself as '*Charles Dickens, Français Naturalisé, et Citoyen de Paris*'. He had holidayed in France with the family on many occasions, generally staying at Boulogne in properties owned by a M. Boucourt-Mutuel. The last family trip was in 1856, and he made no further visits until June 1862 when he went to Paris and stayed for about a month. He was back in Paris by October of 1862, but the few letters that are known refer mainly to the Hausmannian reconstruction of Paris that was in full swing at that time. He was back in England for Christmas, and on 6 January 1863 he wrote from Gad's Hill to Sir Joseph Olliffe, who was the physician at the British Embassy at Paris, referring to coming to Paris via

Above left: The author at the grave of Ellen Ternan. (Author's own)

Above right: The grave of Ellen's sisters, Maria and Frances. (Author's own)

Right: The grave of Maria Winter, nee Beadnel. (Author's own)

These three graves are within meters of each other in the Highland Road Cemetery at Portsmouth. The house in which Dickens was born is less than 4km from these graves. Pure coincidence?

Charles Dickens's birthplace. (Author's own)

MR. CHARLES DICKENS'S LAST READING.

Right: Dickens giving the last reading of his Works. (Wellcome Collection)

Below: The Free Trade Hall, Manchester.

Oliver Twist (*Oliver Twist,* 1838), Dickens first real novel, with the first illegitimate child, Oliver Twist, as the main character. Mrs Ternan is pregnant with Ellen. (George Cruikshank)

Above: Nicholas and The Crummles Family (*Nicholas Nickleby*, 1838–39). The Crummles family of Mr, Mrs and children could well be a reflection of the Ternan family. (CC BY 2.0, Fondo Antiguo de la Biblioteca de la Universidad de Sevilla)

Right: Little Nelly Trent, (*Old Curiosity Shop* 1841). Nell's age is not mentioned with any precision, but she is clearly still a young child. Ellen, frequently referred to as Nelly, is 2 to 3 years old.

Florence Dombey (*Dombey and Son,* 1846–48). Florence about 10 years old and is very much neglected by her father. Ellen is 7 to 8 years old.

Esther Summerson (*Bleak House,* 1852–53) Esther is about 13 years old when she enters the book, and is the illegitimate daughter of Mr Nemo, a lowly copying clerk in a small legal office. Ellen is also that age. Dickens was previously employed as a clerk in a legal office.

Lucie Manette (*Tale of Two Cities*, 1859). Lucie is 18 years old, and for all that time has believed her father to be dead. However, she eventually discovers the truth, that her father is still alive. Ellen is also 18 years old, and her mother's husband is dead, when Ellen meets Charles Dickens.

Bella Wilfer and her father (*Our Mutual Friend*, 1864–65). Bella is about 20 years old, and very close to her father, much as Ellen has a very close relationship with Dickens.

visiting a sick friend. Then on 18 January 1863, he wrote again to Olliffe referring to his own anxiety and sleeplessness. He also wrote to Wilkie Collins in a similar vein on 20 January, and while no names were mentioned in any of these letters, it is generally believed that he was referring to Ellen, and her sickness assumed to be a pregnancy that ended badly. There is, of course, no evidence to support that belief. But that absence of evidence has never stopped the speculation!

He later wrote another letter to Wilkie, but making mention only of Parisian life in general; and a letter to Frederic Ouvry advising that he would be in Paris until the following Wednesday, then travelling for ten to fourteen days prior to returning to the home and office for good. Two letters written on 1 February, one to Mary Dickens and one to Wills, both confirmed that arrangement; that he would be home after ten days to a fortnight.

When his brother Alfred died, Dickens provided a house for his widow Helen and her five children to live in, and perhaps in gratitude and by way of thanks, Helen took in and looked after Dickens's mother at the end of her life. In September 1863 his mother died, having been living for some time in 'a state of bodily and mental decay'. He does not appear to have grieved her passing, and it is doubtful whether he ever did 'forgive or forget' that she was warm for him to continue at the blacking factory. Both she and her late husband had for many years been a drain on Dickens's purse.

The next trip Dickens made to Paris was in June 1864, and while a letter to Wills refers to what Dickens has called 'one of my Mysterious Disappearances', it mostly refers to his latest short story in the *Mrs Lirriper* series and tells us nothing about the 'Mysterious Disappearances' which are probably visits to Ellen and her mother.

Dickens was in Paris again in late May and early June 1865, and his return journey included the train which crashed at Staplehurst in Kent. An innovation in the scheduling of trains between London and the Channel port town of Folkestone provided for what became known as the Tidal Trains. People travelling between London and Paris on the regular trains were obliged to wait for the cross-channel ferries which came and went with the tide. The Tidal Trains travelled at a different time each day, to synchronise with the arrival and departure of the ferries. On 9 June 1865, maintenance work was being carried out on the London–Folkestone rail line, but the workers had forgotten, or had misread, the varying times of the Tidal Trains. Accordingly, without any warning, the train from Folkestone ran into the rail works on the viaduct at about 30 mph, and plunged about three metres into the River Beult below, killing ten and injuring about forty of the 120 or so passengers and crew on board. Dickens was in one of the first-class carriages which miraculously teetered on the brink, but did not actually end up on the river bed. There were two other passengers in the compartment with him, believed to be Ellen and Mrs Ternan. Or perhaps they were the Compact Enchantress and Mystery returning home from *A Flight*? In any event, Dickens helped them safely clamber out, before returning into the compartment to retrieve the manuscript of the next part of *Our Mutual Friend* on which he had been working at the time. Ellen sustained some damage to her arm and, it seems, also lost a bracelet, but Mrs Ternan escaped unharmed. Dickens, in his usual way, went among the injured offering them brandy from his hip flask, probably doing more harm than good. A special replacement train was sent to collect those able to get aboard, and they were taken to London.

Life then settled back to normal, with Ellen and her mother disappearing into the mists, and Dickens getting back to work, including finishing *Our Mutual Friend* and conducting his reading tours in America in 1867, and around England. But all this was to take its toll. His health was not in a particularly good state, and halfway through writing *The Mystery of Edwin Drood* he collapsed and died on 9 June 1870, five years to the day of the Staplehurst train crash. His funeral was held in Westminster Abbey on 19 June, just ten days after his death. An estimated 10,000 people lined the route of the funeral procession, but there were only a handful of mourners allowed into the Abbey for the actual service, these being mostly family members. Dickens had always maintained that he wanted no fuss at his death, rather, he just wanted to be buried in some unostentatious corner somewhere, perhaps at Rochester. The limited number of mourners was in accordance with that wish, but he couldn't escape Poet's Corner in the Abbey. He was too important an English writer by far not to be placed there.

Following the funeral, as usually happens after any massive out-pouring of public grief, life very quickly went back to normal. And it pretty much remained that way until Wright and Storey published their books some sixty-five years after Dickens's death.

Chapter Six

The Last Four Novels

Any interpretation of the last four novels not taking Ellen into account, would be awry
                    Thomas Wright, *The Life of Dickens*

Let us turn now to the last four novels, the first of which was *A Tale of Two Cities*, published in 1859. Set in France and England at the time of the French Revolution, it tells the story of Lucie Manette, an apparently orphaned 18-year-old young woman who travels to Paris and finally meets her father, Doctor Manette, presumed to have died shortly after Lucie's birth. However, he had been incarcerated in the Bastille for eighteen years but has now been freed and is able to travel to London through the agency of a Mr Lorry of Telson's Bank. Travelling on the same cross-channel ferry is a French man, Charles Darnay, who is arrested on arrival in England and put on trial, accused of being a French spy. However, Darnay is acquitted on the arguments of his lawyer's assistant Sidney Carton on the basis of 'mistaken identity', both men looking very much alike. Both Charles and Sydney fall in love with Lucie, who marries Charles with whom she then has a daughter, also named Lucie. Eventually, Sydney Carton sacrifices his own life to save that of Charles Darnay in order that Lucy's happiness in her marriage continues.

Throughout the story, Lucie develops her relationship with the father she had always believed to be dead. In the preface to the first edition of *A Tale of Two Cities* Dickens writes:

> When I was acting, with my children and friends, in Mr Wilkie Collins's drama of *The Frozen Deep*, I first conceived the main idea of this story. A strong desire was upon me then, to embody it in my own person; and I traced out in my fancy, the state of mind of which it would necessitate the presentation to an observant spectator, with particular care and interest.
>
> As the idea became familiar to me, it gradually shaped itself into its present form. Throughout its execution, it has had complete possession of me; I have so far verified what is done and suffered in these pages, as that I have certainly done and suffered it all myself.
>
> Whenever any reference (however slight) is made here to the condition of the French people before or during the Revolution, it is truly made, on the faith of trustworthy witnesses. It has been one of my hopes to add something to the popular and picturesque means of understanding that terrible time, though no one can hope to add anything to the philosophy of Mr Carlyle's wonderful book.

It is very clear from the opening chapter that the 'main idea' of the story would be the French Revolution, but there is no apparent reason why that should have come so readily into

Dickens's mind while acting in *The Frozen Deep*. If that is not the 'main idea', it would certainly have to be considered as the main 'setting' for the story, and if that is so, the 'main idea' to which Dickens was referring, and which might have come into his mind at that time, could possibly have reflected the triangle of Richard Wardour, Frank Aldersley and Clara Burnham.

Loosely based on the ill-fated 1845 Franklin expedition to find the North West Passage through the Arctic ice cap, the romantic plot of the play *The Frozen Deep* involves Miss Clara Burnham, who is the beloved of two members of the expeditionary crew: Richard Wardour and Frank Aldersley. Clara has become enamoured with Aldersley, but is blissfully unaware that Wardour and Aldersley are bitter rivals for her affection. After a considerable time has elapsed with no news from the expedition, it is feared that the two ships have come to grief in the ice, and a rescue mission is mounted to search for the missing crews. Clara travels with them, and while the party are waiting for news at Newfoundland, Wardour struggles through the ice and snow, nearly dead from exhaustion, bringing the news that he has carried Aldersley, also near death, to the rescue station, and he is just outside. Wardour dies in Clara's arms, but her lover, Aldersley has been saved, thanks to the heroic efforts of Wardour.

In the gradual shaping of the story, the competition between Charles Darnay and Sydney Carton for the love of Lucie Manette would have emerged, the result of course being Carton's self-sacrifice, mirroring that of Richard Wardour. But neither the French Revolution nor the self-sacrifices of Carton and Wardour would fall into the description of 'that I have certainly done and suffered it all myself'. In all the biographies I have read, I have not come across one example of Dickens sacrificing himself in order to save the life of a rival in love.

However, another 'main idea' is obviously the 'recalling to life' of Dr Manette. Shortly after Lucie's conception, and prior to her birth, Dr Manette was incarcerated in the Bastille, and remained there for the better part of eighteen years. During that time, Mrs Manette delivered her child Lucie, but died two years later. Lucie was raised through the agency of Tellson's Bank, and for sixteen of her eighteen years believed herself to be an orphan. But, again through the agency of Tellson's Bank, Lucie discovers her father is not dead, and much of the story then rotates around Dr Manette's rehabilitation and the relationship with his daughter following their first meeting in the Defarge apartment. If my thesis is correct, then here we do have a circumstance through which Dickens 'has done and suffered' himself. While Dickens was not incarcerated in a stone-walled prison like the Bastille, he was certainly bound by the bonds of matrimony through the whole of Ellen's life from her conception to finally meeting her eighteen years later. And perhaps this is a timely place to remember Ackroyd's assertion that in late 1838 (i.e. shortly after Ellen's conception) Dickens appeared to have been 'chaffing against the strains of domesticity – a sense of wishing to break away from bonds'.

From the age of 7, following the death of her mother's husband, Ellen had believed her father to be dead. And just as Lucie Manette had to come to terms with her father still being alive, so also did Ellen. Thus, I believe that in *A Tale of Two Cities*, Dickens, through the story of Dr Manette and Lucie, is telling the story of Ellen and himself, and that is the 'main idea' that came into Dickens's fancy during the performances of *The Frozen Deep* and, especially, of *Uncle John*. The time lapse between the conception of both young women, and their age at which they met and began to get to know their biological fathers, being almost exactly eighteen years in both cases, is surely more than just coincidence.

It is tempting to think that perhaps Lucie, both mother and/or daughter, might have had some part of Dickens's childhood sweetheart Lucy Stroughill embedded within them. Whether that is the case or not is irrelevant. The characters themselves are not important in this analysis; rather it is the relationship between the characters that is. Writing a novel with a developing father/daughter relationship at its core at this tumultuous time in Dickens's life seems to be very deliberate on his part.

(Here I believe it is important to acknowledge that the Irish writer Cora Harrison had, quite independently, come to this same conclusion having read *A Tale of Two Cities*. This had been brought to my attention after the publication of my 2022 paper 'Illegitimacy in Dickens, and the Riddle of Ellen Ternan' in *The Dickensian*, in which I first discussed the possibility that Ellen was Dickens's daughter rather than his mistress. It was also after the manuscript for this book was well advanced. Harrison had not published her article in a journal, but rather on her personal website, (Summer of Secrets – Cora Harrison) which is why I had not discovered it.)

In 1860/61 Dickens wrote *Great Expectations*. Based on very little more than the similarity of the names, Estella and Ellen, Thomas Wright appeared to be convinced that one was based on the other. In terms of just their names, he may have been correct. But in terms of relationships I think he was very much awry. Admittedly we know very little of Ellen, but in what we do know I see very little of Estella in her, apart from her name and her illegitimacy. Beyond that, even Estella's parentage is quite different to Ellen's. If Estella had been based on anyone in particular, I would say there is a lot more of Maria Beadnell than of Ellen Ternan woven into her. The long, but agonisingly fruitless pursuance of Estella by Pip, is a strong reflection of Dickens's failed pursuance of Maria. Dickens used expressions such as her 'cold-hearted indifference' and his own 'wretchedness' and such like, both in his final letters to Maria, and in his writing of Estella's treatment of Pip. Despite Pip's pleadings, Estella chooses to marry Bentley Drummle, while Maria abandons Dickens to marry the banker, Mr Winter. But after some considerable time apart, Pip and Estella meet again, just as do Maria Winter and Dickens. However, neither of the two meetings provide the hoped-for restoration of affection, and Dickens's disappointment in Mrs Winter is reflected in the difficulty he had in providing a satisfactory conclusion to *Great Expectations*. So, in *Great Expectations* there is no character reflecting a child of Dickens's imagination; and there never have been any appearances in his novels of the legitimate children of his flesh.

But that is not the case in the next novel, *Our Mutual Friend*, written in 1864/65. At this time, Ellen was living partly in France, and of course it was on the way home from there that they were involved in the Tidal Train crash at Staplehurst, in which they could so easily have perished themselves, and part of the manuscript of *Our Mutual Friend* could have been lost. But they didn't, and it wasn't. But of course the name

Bella was linked to that of Ellen by Thomas Wright, leading to Harrison declaring Ellen to be 'Dickens's greedy little gold-digging mistress', which in turn led me to seek a different portrait of her. While I can quite see that Ellen might well have expressed the view that, like Bella, she hated being poor and wanted money, it should be noted that Bella was actually speaking at that time with her father, not with a lover. In light of that, if we are going to draw a parallel between Bella and Ellen, we should see that conversation being between Ellen and her father, not between a mistress and her lover. Ellen had, for the decade prior to *Uncle John*, been living in very precarious circumstances. Her widowed mother, while popular as an actress, would only have been paid for hours on stage, which would have meant an uncertain financial situation for the family of four. They would have been living in lodgings and frequently travelling around, following opportunities for work. Under those circumstances, it would not be at all surprising had Ellen, in talking with Dickens, mentioned how much she had disliked, even 'hated', being poor. So what we have in the loving and playful relationship between Bella and her father in *Our Mutual Friend*, is a novel that includes for the first time, a child of Dickens's flesh actually with her father. Maybe I am being fanciful but it does, I think, support the daughter hypothesis rather than the mistress.

Can we winkle anything out of the last, unfinished novel, *The Mystery of Edwin Drood*? Once again we have a name similarity in Helena Landless. We do have a Mystery. But will we find Compact Enchantress? I think not. Dickens has expiated his mistakes making adequate provision for Catherine and her children, and for Mrs Ternan and Ellen. His troubled conscience is now relieved. After writing:

> Mrs Tope's care has spread a very neat, clean breakfast ready for her lodger. Before sitting down to it, he opens his corner-cupboard door; takes his bit of chalk from its shelf; adds one thick line to the score, extending from the top of the cupboard door to the bottom; and then falls to with an appetite.

Dickens laid down his pen and he was dead. There would be nothing more from his pen for us to read other than what was written earlier, but which would come to light later. Maybe there is still more to be found, perhaps even some very revealing letters. But in the meantime, we simply have to make do with what we have to hand.

Chapter Seven

Ellen 1870–1913

Come live with mee, and be my love, And we will all the pleasures prove,
That Vallies, groves, hills and fieldes, Woods, or steepie mountaine yeeldes

Christopher Marlowe
The passionate Sheepheard to his love

Dickens was dead and his burial had been witnessed by fourteen mourners, of which only thirteen had been named in the 'official' list. It is almost certain that the fourteenth, unnamed mourner was Ellen, and why not indeed? Had she been his mistress for the last twelve years of his life that would have been understandable. If she were his daughter, albeit illegitimate, that would have been natural, right and proper. If it were not Ellen, I am not even going to guess who else it might have been, but certainly I would have expected her to be there, and very surprised were she not.

The question for Ellen now was 'what am I to do next?' I am not going to speculate on her financial situation beyond the £1,000.00 she is known to have inherited from Dickens. She may have been drawing some income from the property, Houghton House, Ampthill, that was apparently purchased for her a few years prior to Dickens's death, and she might have accumulated some savings during these last few years, being supported by Dickens. But I doubt that there would have been much in the way of savings from the years 'on the road' as travelling players. Her eldest sister, Fanny, was now financially independent as the wife of Thomas Adolphus Trollope, and as a writer. The middle sister, Maria, had gained an independent life first as the wife of a brewer's son, one William Rowland Taylor, whom she married in 1863. Following her divorce a decade later she attended the Slade School of Art before moving to Italy and travelling in North Africa. She was a competent writer, and, unusually for that time, worked as a journalist for the *London Standard* for over a decade. But at the time of the death of Dickens, Maria was still with her husband, and it was there, at The Lawns in Oxford, that Mrs Ternan and her three daughters initially congregated.

But Ellen was now independent, and perhaps could spread her wings a little. Of Dickens's two other daughters, Mary never married, and had lived all her life to this stage at home. Katey had married a decade earlier when she reached the age of 21 and could marry without parental consent. Katey herself was to later report her father as saying that if it were not for him, (that is to say, his behaviour), 'Katey would never have left home'. Whereas all the male children were chuffed off to various places including Germany and Boulogne, at quite tender ages, the daughters appear to have been kept on much tighter reins. It is quite likely, then, that Ellen was also 'protected' in this way through the period 1858 to 1870, and now came to relish the thought of a little freedom. By 1870 of course, she was already 31, and perhaps feeling a little 'on the shelf'. However, she had retained her youthful looks and was able to take a decade off, quoting her age as 21. It has been speculated that she did this to 'wipe out' the decade with Dickens. However, it is equally possible that it was the ten years on the road following Mr Ternan's death in the asylum for the insane that she would have liked to wipe out. After all, it could not have been an easy time, travelling with her widowed mother and her sisters, living on the precarious income earned collectively by the four of them. By all accounts Ellen was not the best actor of the family, and probably was only engaged for the much smaller roles, and frequently dressed up as a male character. She was born into the profession, rather than choosing it for herself, but being born into it does not mean that she necessarily enjoyed it. But it was all she knew, and all she could do. Today, youngsters wishing to take to the stage can study drama at high school, and go on to university or to drama colleges for degree-level studies. No such opportunities were available to Ellen, so it was necessary to make the best she could, and just get on with it.

But now she was free, and maybe reduced her age by a decade for no reason other than because she could. Certainly one advantage of this would have been to greatly increase the size and depth of the gene pool in which she could paddle in search of an eligible young man, someone who could give her the type of love that had so far been denied her. Whatever her thoughts and strategies were, she pretty soon took herself off to the Continent, perhaps 'to find herself' and to give serious consideration to her future. While there she met and formed a friendship with one Rosalind Brown, a recent widow and perhaps also a lost soul seeking some consolation in her bereavement. Rosalind Brown had apparently inherited a house in Kensington, and suggested to Ellen that when back in England, she would be very welcome as a paying guest. Rosalind would later become an important part of Ellen's life, and Ellen would be very grateful to her. Meanwhile, Ellen spent quite some time on the Continent, eventually returning to England in the summer of 1871. At this time it seems that Maria and Frances had also left The Lawn, leaving only Mrs Ternan and her son-in-law, Maria's husband, in situ; but by summer Maria was also back.

Ellen was by now ready to jump into the gene pool to look for a suitable mate, and as it happened – through some distant relative – Maria and Ellen were invited to a party at Queen's College during 'Eights Week', where their host, second year student George Wharton Robinson, was rowing on that very pool. Who was first attracted to whom is not clear, but apparently George and Ellen 'hit it off' immediately. It is possible that Ellen was initially attracted to George's name, perhaps having read, and remembered, one of Dickens's last short stories, *George Silverman's Explanation*, written in 1868. After a diabolically bad childhood, George Silverman eventually took holy orders and was given a preferment at a small living on the estate of Lady Fareway. This Lady had a daughter, Adelina, who was everything that could be wished for, and George fell in love with her. However, George had a student, Granville Wharton, who also fell in love with Adelina. The story then becomes the one in *The Frozen Deep* and *A Tale of Two Cities*, whereby one suitor, in this case George Silverman, gives up the girl in order that the other might carry off the prize. In fact, the Rev. George Silverman actually secretly performs the marriage ceremony and not only loses the girl for his troubles, but also loses his job. Whether or not this played any part in Ellen's attraction to George Wharton Robinson is irrelevant. The fact remains that for a short while they were attracted to each other.

But after the summer Ellen returned to Italy, where she seems to have stayed for about a year, returning to England by the onset of winter 1872. In November she then suffered a breakdown of some sort, almost certainly a reoccurrence of the episode she suffered in 1861–2, wrongly, I believe, diagnosed as a pregnancy. It has been suggested that the breakdown this time was precipitated by some 'rough handling' by publisher George Smith after she had tried, unsuccessfully, to persuade Smith to publish a poem by Alfred Austin. However, if one looks at the timelines, the first episode came on about three years following the upheaval to her life when the close association with Dickens (whatever that association might have been) began, and this one came on about three years after the upheaval caused by Dickens's death.

Whatever the cause, she retired to Eastbourne for a spell of good sea air, where she was joined by her sister Frances. The two returned to Oxford for Christmas, but Ellen continued to be unwell. In February, Frances returned to Italy, and Ellen was advised to once again leave Oxford, retreating on this occasion to Brighton. At this stage, Maria and her husband separated, and the 70-year-old Mrs Ternan was suffering from bronchitis, not helped by Oxford's cold and damp climate. Mrs Ternan died in October 1873, and shortly after, Maria left her husband for good.

Re-enter Rosalind Brown. With no family around, Ellen became a frequent guest with Mrs Brown; her health was still very far from good, even though Tomalin believed there was nothing fundamentally wrong with her. There may not have been anything physically wrong with Ellen, but I have no doubt that she was suffering from an acute mental health problem, and of course, at that time there were no treatments such as serotonin reuptake inhibitors or antidepressants available which could have been prescribed by her doctor. Thus, all he was able to do was to recommend rest.

But she did recover and after another spell in Italy returned to Rosalind Brown's house in England, from where, on 31 January 1876, she married George Wharton Robinson. By this time, George had graduated and had been ordained as a deacon. Perhaps encouraged by Ellen, George gave up parish work and they moved to the East Kent coastal town of Margate where George would be Headmaster of a private school for boys. That school is long gone, but College Square remains and has been redeveloped as a supermarket.

While at Margate Ellen became the perfect wife of the Headmaster. She was very active in the school, including teaching spelling, and encouraging the boys to participate in theatrical activities. She was also very active in various charitable groups, and certainly chipped in with fund-raising activities, among which she gave readings of *A Christmas Carol* and other Dickens books, which were very well received. Clearly her early acting career, and perhaps memory of Dickens himself reading, contributed to the quality of her renditions. While at Margate the Robinsons had two children, Geoffrey and Gladys. Both children were active in Ellen's theatrical productions. It was also at Margate that Ellen met, as a matter of course, with the Reverend William Benham, then the vicar at

St John's Church. Benham was a Dickens enthusiast, who had at one time been a vice-president of the Dickens Fellowship, and was also known for his local charitable public readings of Dickens. Thus, it was quite likely that Ellen became involved in the charities through Benham. And it was this same William Benham whom Thomas Wright of Olney later claimed had told him about Ellen's 'confession' about having been Dickens's mistress. All that needs to be said about that claim has already been covered in every biography about Charles Dickens with the exception of that by John Forster, and I do not need to add any more, other than to remind people that this whole episode is totally unsubstantiated hearsay. Benham had been dead for twenty-five years before Wright made his announcement, so no one was able to confirm with Benham quite what he did say to Wright   While everything appeared to be going very well for the Robinson family at Margate, matters started going pear-shaped when, in March 1886, George suddenly became unwell with some unspecified medical problem, the treatment for which required him to rest. Since that was pretty much the advice given to Ellen in 1874, and since there had not been much progress in the way of treating mental health issues in that intervening twelve years, it would be reasonable to suppose it was a mental health problem. George gave up his role as a magistrate, the school was sold at a considerable loss, and the family moved back to London, taking lodgings in the same house as Rosalind Wickham, previously Mrs Brown, with whom Ellen had lodged prior to her marriage.

All of this history, and of Ellen's history up to her death at age 75 in 1914 is very clearly set out in Claire Tomalin's *Invisible Woman*, and I admit that I am very grateful for, and have relied heavily on, that work for most of the general information about Ellen's life. I cannot fault Tomalin's research, it is only her interpretations that are quite clearly too much influenced by the Wright/Storey narrative that I have difficulty accepting. Having said that, there is little need for me to repeat details of Ellen's life here in any great detail. Suffice to say that following periods of market gardening, small teaching jobs and the like, George's health declined and he died. Ellen's sisters aged gracefully at Southsea, and there they died, Maria in 1903 and Fanny in 1913. Despite her own ailing health (she had cancer) Ellen survived another year and died in 1914. She is buried in Portsmouth Cemetery, ironically only a few metres away from the mortal remains of Maria Winter, née Beadnell.

From a close study of all that happened with respect to Ellen from the time she left Margate, there is absolutely nothing that takes one any closer to the truth about her relationship to Charles Dickens. It has been noted by many commentators that Ellen never made any allusion to her past life with Dickens. But why would she? There would have been absolutely nothing for her to gain from talking about it, whether she was his mistress or his daughter. For her to publicly raise the possibility of her being his mistress would have brought her nothing but calumny. And as for claiming to have been his daughter, unless she had some unknown authentic document signed by Dickens himself, she would have had no more proof of that than all of those who have written about her, myself included.

It might also be asked why Forster made no comment about Ellen in his biography of Dickens. He was very clearly aware of the true situation, and had he written her into his *Life of Dickens* (1872–4) perhaps there would have been no mystery about her today. He knew what an important person she was in Dickens's life but nonetheless wrote her out, apart from the inclusion of Dickens's Last Will and Testament. I think his leaving her out may have had a lot more to do with Ellen, her husband and children still being alive, rather than being a conspiracy with the general Dickens family to not sully his name. Forster's book was about Dickens the author, not about Ellen the actress. To have written anything at all about her without mentioning the relationship between them would have been difficult to do without in some way damaging her reputation, perhaps even in the eyes of her husband if she had not previously explained it to him. And that is something that I think John Forster simply would not have done. But he could not leave her out entirely, so chose the simplicity of just including the Will.

Here, as we have just considered what Ellen might, or might not have said about her relationship with Dickens, and what Forster maybe could have said but didn't, let us briefly consider what Ellen's mother and her sisters Frances and Maria might have thought and said. After all, Mrs Ternan was living pretty comfortably being funded by Dickens, as were the two elder daughters prior to their marriages. How would their consciences have been pricked, knowing that the assistance they were receiving from Dickens was being paid for by the sexual favours Ellen was bestowing on him? In *The Invisible Woman*, Tomalin opines that there had to be an innocent version of Nelly's activities that the family could use, if necessary, to satisfy any curious friends, and even their own consciences.[31] Tomalin then suggests a version along the lines of Dickens simply being a close friend of the family, and devoted to them all, but Ellen being more like a daughter to him, and reciprocating his affection with a true, daughterly devotion. This is of course very similar to the *Uncle John* script. Being the excellent, experienced professional biographer that Claire Tomalin undoubtedly is, and usually being very particular and meticulous in providing references for what she asserts, it is interesting to note that she gives no reference for the origin of this statement. One is left to assume that this is a script concocted by Tomalin herself, rather than thought out and used by the family. Now I find it ironic that Claire Tomalin has presented us with a 'fiction' that the family might have used about the relationship, that is more like the truth as I see it, in order to explain what she has always accepted as a 'truth', but what I see as more of a fiction!

Just as Peter Ackroyd and Angus Wilson before her, she has come so close to thinking about a father/daughter relationship but again, apparently without actually investigating it as a possibility. Rather, she has served it up as being an untruth that might just enable others to gloss over the accepted 'truth', that Ellen was his mistress.

Chapter Eight

The Search for Evidence is On!

It was in the book, and at that we'd let it go, for we never could believe that print would lie.
>Henry Lawson; *The Old Bark School*

After Wright had brought the matter of Ellen being Dickens's mistress into the public domain once more in 1935, and then Storey chipping in with her claim in 1939 that Ellen had borne his child, it was on again for young and old. With very few exceptions, everyone immediately, and unquestioningly, believed the new narrative, and all wished to be the one who found the evidence to confirm it. Of course, as we know, everyone has failed miserably in those endeavours but they still cling on, and with very few exceptions, will not hear a word spoken against it. One of the non-believers was Edward Wagenknecht, who, in the early 1950s, challenged the story on the grounds of the total lack of evidence. Wagenknecht[32] attacked what he saw as very sloppy, even irresponsible, scholarship, with the unverifiable claims reported as facts; an attack for which he received a public reprimand from the then Doyenne of Dickensian scholarship, Ada Nisbet.

It was almost certainly the outspoken Edward Wagenknecht whom Ada Nisbet had in her sights when she wrote the preface to her book *Dickens and Ellen Ternan*, (1952)[33] in which she refers to:

the violence of certain recent attacks upon the reliability and integrity of those critics and scholars who have accepted the story of Dickens's liaison with Ellen Ternan as fact. The attackers claim there is no 'evidence'. I have gathered an accumulation of what I am convinced constitutes 'evidence'. I respect the critics and writers under fire who include such people as Dame Una Pope-Hennessy, Hesketh Pearson, Edmund Wilson, Lionel Stevenson, Clifton Fadiman and W. Somerset Maugham among others, and I resent the nature and tone of the attacks.

Well, I am sorry Ada, what you have gathered is evidence of a strong bond between Charles Dickens and Ellen Ternan, but it is by no means evidence of a consummated sexual relationship. Professor Wagenknecht was quite right in his criticisms. One cannot simply 'accept as fact' that which is not supported by evidence, however 'respected' the critics and writers might be.

Another, more recent doubter was Peter Ackroyd. In his biography *Dickens*, as mentioned earlier in Chapter Two, he expressed the view that it was very unlikely that the relationship was consummated, and to provide a reason for Dickens's behaviour at the time gave a very deep, and I thought rather convoluted, Freudian psychoanalytic explanation.

There were many theories, or rather excuses, as to why no evidence could be found. The baby was not registered. It was registered under false names. It was registered in France and the records destroyed in the Commune of 1871, or in the First World War, or in the Second World War. It was registered somewhere so out of the way it could never be found. And so it goes on. If you apply Ockham's Razor,[34] the only reasonable explanation for the absence of evidence that would emerge is because there was no baby born in 1862, or any other time, dead or alive.

I have already mentioned a couple of letters written by Dickens in 1862 in which he refers to his being 'unsettled' and 'anxious' and to visiting, in France, a 'friend who has been suffering a long and lonely ordeal'. The friend, not unreasonably, has been identified as Ellen. But 'the long and lonely ordeal' has been diagnosed as proof of the pregnancy that resulted in the child who died. Rather a pretty long bow to draw. Surely no one reading a letter referring to visiting a sick friend who had been suffering a long and lonely ordeal, would think of it as a pregnancy, with or without a bad outcome, unless they were prejudiced by the previous claim of the birth of a child, but which died.

Similarly, the story of Bebelle, published in 1862, has also been used to confirm the original diagnosis. When Storey broke the news about the baby who died, there was no clue as to when or where this happened, or how the baby died. In his book *Charles Dickens and the Great Theatre of the World*,[35] Simon Callow writes of the possibility that at some point Ellen became pregnant and went to France for an abortion. I give credit to Callow for using the word 'possible', thereby introducing a modicum of doubt.

But nobody (apart, I believe, from myself) has ever tried to give an explanation for the 1862 illness other than it being a pregnancy, and here I shall include another example of such an interpretation. In January 1863, Dickens attended a performance in Paris of Gounod's *Faust*. It seems to have made a very great impression on him, and he wrote to Georgina telling her he was dreadfully upset by it, and how it sounded like a mournful echo of things in his own heart. He wrote in a similar vein to Macready, stressing the effectiveness of the set and the lighting. Claire Tomalin, unable (or perhaps unwilling?) to think of any other plausible explanation, believes he was writing of himself and Ellen.

To a certain extent I am inclined to agree with Tomalin in this interpretation, but there is a major weakness as it stands, and there *is* an alternative. While Tomalin refers to the role played by some jewellery (an echo of Dickens's gift of trinkets to Ellen?) in Faust's debauchery of Marguerite and fate of the resultant child, she does not mention that it is the rejuvenated Faust that is in action, not the elderly man.

In Act One of the opera, the aging scholar, Faust, comes to the depressing conclusion that through his entire life, his studies and work have amounted to nothing and have only resulted in him missing out on life and love. Twice he attempts to kill himself with poison but stops each time when he hears a choir singing which provides a fleeting moment of optimism. He curses hope and faith, and asks for infernal guidance whereupon Mephistopheles appears with a tempting image of the beautiful and pure Marguerite at her spinning wheel. He persuades Faust to buy his services on Earth in exchange for Faust's in Hell. Faust's goblet of poison is magically transformed into an elixir of youth, immediately transforming the aged doctor into a handsome young gentleman. It is this handsome young gentlemanly version of Faust, not the aging Faust, who goes on to tempt Marguerite with a gift of jewellery and debauch her. Thus, in the Paris Opera, Dickens suddenly, and surprisingly, finds himself being confronted by the mournful echo of the indiscretion of his *youthful* self, and it was that 'flashback' in time that was so upsetting, not the current relationship with Ellen. This interpretation is entirely consistent with the notion of Dickens having had an affair with Mrs Ternan back in 'the days you remember…' and being haunted by that memory of wrongdoing as so often indicated through his letters and fiction.

Trying to give a retrospective diagnosis 180 years after the event with no medical evidence is fraught with difficulty. But if we look a little later at Ellen's health after Dickens's death (as described by Claire Tomalin in *The Invisible Woman*) it is very clear that she did experience, at that time, a 'long and lonely ordeal', nursed back to health on this occasion by Rosalind Brown. Ellen's sister Fanny, writing in 1874 to her stepdaughter Bice, said of Ellen that she had no appetite and was failing to regain her strength, and that she had been advised to take complete rest, and not to exert herself for more than a few moments. Subsequent letters indicated her recovery was being stubbornly slow, and she was continuing to suffer. Quite what this year-long problem was, appears to be unknown, but Tomalin states, quite unsympathetically, that there was 'nothing fundamentally wrong with her'. Most probably, then, Ellen was suffering a nervous illness, perhaps an eating disorder with severe loss of appetite and strength, which took her a year to recover from. Further, in *The Real Ellen Ternan*,[36] Katharine Longley draws attention to Ellen's 'delicate health' and to her being on one occasion 'a nervous wreck seeking treatment from a faith healer'. It is quite possible that these were reoccurrences of the episodes of illness referred to in Dickens's earlier letters – that is to say, that the original 'long and lonely ordeal' was also an episode of mental or nervous illness rather than of pregnancy. It is well documented that loss of freedom can lead to mental illness such as depression. Ellen was being detained, hidden away, deprived of her freedom, kept away from old friends and unable to make new. It must also be remembered that Ellen's life from childhood had not always been easy. Constantly on the move, with no formal schooling, and not staying anywhere long enough to develop a group of her peers as friends and supporters. Biographers have made much of the effect on the young Charles Dickens of his father's incarceration in the Marshalsea for a few months. How much worse would it have been for Ellen to see the person she had believed to be her father locked away in an asylum for the insane when she was 5, never to see him again? This is certainly more than enough to cause mental illness in a sensitive girl in her mid-twenties.

Having jumped from the supposed baby's birth in 1862 to a second 'long and lonely ordeal' that most definitely was not a birth in 1874, let us now go back to another suggested date for the birth of the putative baby, roughly half way between these two episodes of illness, 1867.

Dickens kept a daily diary in which he recorded details of appointments and the like, which he simply destroyed at the end of each year when they were no longer relevant. He would then start a new diary for the current year. It seems that the 1867 diary was lost, perhaps stolen, towards the end of the year while he was in America, before it would have been destroyed, and somehow found its way to an auction in 1922. It remained junked together with other Dickensian memorabilia until 1943, a few years following the Wright/Storey publications when everyone was re-evaluating such material. It is such a small diary, measuring only about 10cm by 5cm, that there is room for only a few characters to be written into any one day's allocated space. I have not seen the original, but it is available from the digital collections of the New York Public Library,[37] from where this image of the page for April 1867 has been downloaded.

On this page for April there are entries which include the words 'Arrival', 'Loss', 'Wills', and across the bottom of the page, 'N. ill latter part of this month'. Putting them together into some sort of narrative, it has been suggested that the 'Illness' is related to a pregnancy, 'Arrival' to a birth, 'Loss' to a death, and the presence of 'Wills' as his being there to help with it all. Dickens's writing is necessarily small and cramped due to the lack of space, but the entry for 13 April which includes the word 'arrival' reads:

'To Sl:at 10.25. at Sl: at $2^{1/2}$ Arrival'.

That for 19 April which includes the name of Wills reads:

'At Off: (undecipheral squiggle) To Sl: (Wills) at $2^{1/2}$'

And that for 20 April which includes the word [Loss] reads:

'To Off from Sl at 11.40 [Loss]'. To GH

So as I read it, 'arrival', coupled as it is with the $2^{1/2}$ is simply that Dickens, not a baby, will arrive at Slough at half past two on 13 April. This is the same with Wills – he will also arrive at Slough at 2.30, that is to say on the same train, but on the 19th. The financial year in England ends on 5 April, and Wills is Dickens's man of business. Most likely then, Wills is at Slough not to assist in some way with a mysterious birth, but to finalise the 1866–7 accounts. On profit and loss statements, any loss is always enclosed in [square brackets], and if the accounts had shown that any of Dickens's activities had made a loss for the year, he most likely would have noted that disappointing result in his diary. Having said that, the fact that Dickens simply destroyed his diaries at the end of the year when they were no longer relevant, it would be reasonable to think that the vast majority of the entries were not of the 'Dear Diary' type which are aides-memoire of significant events or innermost thoughts. More likely they were prospective notes to remind him of things to be done and places to be, rather than records of events already past. One can see from Dickens's letters, which included a meeting or social event such as a dinner, very precise times were very frequently stated. Clearly Dickens was a stickler for punctuality, and the entries in his diary were to make sure that he was never the one to arrive late.

Dickens was also noted for his powers of memory. He would not have needed to record in his diary such a significant event as the birth and death of a child. As for Ellen's illness, the chances are it was just that. London and its environs was a pretty unhealthy place to live: less than a decade earlier Londoners had experienced the Great Stink, and while Bazelgette had made some progress with reconstructing the sewers from 1862, by 1867 it was still not very far advanced. The Thames and all other sources of water were still open sewers, and any lapse in food handling hygiene could very quickly result in a nasty gut upset. It is also interesting to note that Ellen was again ill on 20 May of this year, as shown in this extract from the diary.

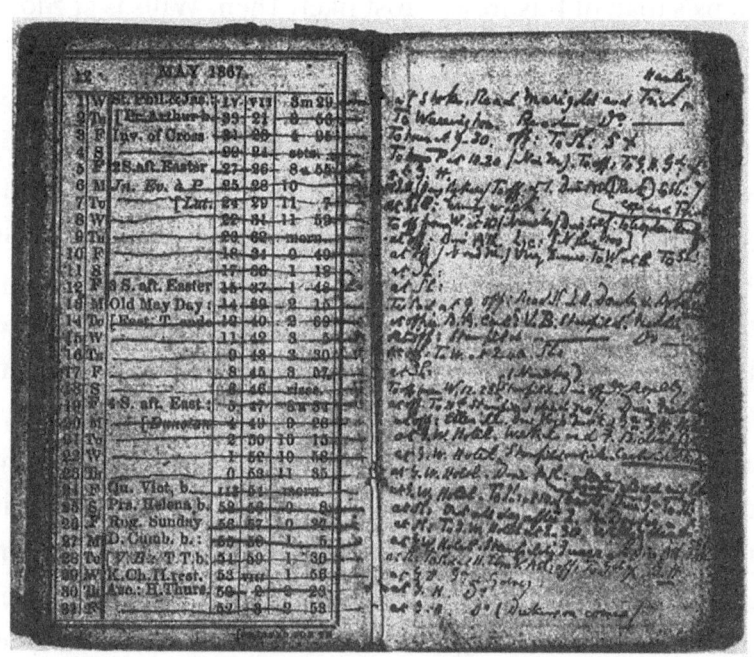

Only those with an undying belief in the Wright/Storey narrative and seeking the elusive evidence, would take those four words in isolation and out of context, to arrive at a diagnosis of a second pregnancy having gone wrong, especially as there is no actual evidence of any previous pregnancy whether it ended badly or not. In relation to Ellen's illnesses, and to the cryptic notes in the diary, Tomalin exhorts us to keep an open mind on the subject, because there is at least the possibility that Ellen could have become pregnant more than once. She goes on to claim that it would be wrong to dismiss that possibility out of hand as long as the 'Arrival' and 'Loss' entries in the diary remain unexplained.

But there is another entry on the April page indicating an arrival, the penultimate line just above the entry telling of Nelly's illness. True it is abbreviated to 'arr', but if we are expected to accept that the first arrival is of a child, then what should we make of this second arrival? Nobody else has commented on it, but it looks to me as though it refers to the train that arrives at 9.30. Surely not another birth! And the entry for 20 May indicates once again that Ellen is ill. Surely not another pregnancy!

I believe the explanation I have given above should be quite sufficient to allow us to 'dismiss the possibility', not so much out of hand, but by providing a much simpler and realistic explanation for those particular diary entries. I shall make no comment whatsoever on 'keeping an open mind', other than to suggest that an open mind has certainly not been maintained at all in relation to the whole Gladys Storey story! It is also interesting to ask why Katey was unaware of, and never mentioned, a second birth. The answer, of course, is because there probably was no birth at all!

Other snippets of information gleaned from this small diary were the keys to the mystery of the correspondence between Dickens and Wills prior to his trip to America. While making his plans for the trip, Dickens and Wills entered into a 'conspiracy' about whether Ellen would, or would not, travel with him. Letters between the two men indicated that while there would be problems with taking Ellen (obviously he could not take her as either his mistress or his illegitimate daughter), Dickens did make plans to assess the situation once he arrived there. The letters to Wills referred to codes Dickens would send back with the outcomes of his assessments, and while it all made very little sense to anyone reading the letters to start with, the codes were found on the November pages of the 1867 diary. One code meant that it would be alright for Ellen to join him there, the other meant for her not to go. The diary enabled the interpretation of the message which turned out to be 'do not come'.

It was generally accepted that the whole plan for Ellen to go was Dickens's idea because he could not bear the thought of being away from her for so long. However, anyone who keeps an open mind on their relationship, might see it as Ellen herself wishing to go. Although living quite comfortably, it could not have been much fun for Ellen – living the life of a spinster looking after her ageing mother while her married sisters were gadding about. When Dickens started planning his trip to America in 1867 it would not have been at all surprising if Ellen herself had floated the idea of him taking her. She did have some distant relatives in the States, and would have heard her mother talk about places that she had visited. Her sisters were having adventurous travels, why shouldn't she? Dickens obviously gave consideration to her wishes, and decided he would first travel alone, and if it were possible, Ellen could follow.

For Dickens, however, he would have been in the same cleft stick whether Ellen were his mistress or his illegitimate daughter. How could he have introduced her and explained her presence? Certainly as neither his mistress nor his illegitimate daughter. He would also have needed to take a chaperone/maid for Ellen, and all three would have needed separate accommodation. That, and three fares, would have tripled the cost of the whole venture. His sole purpose for going was to boost his income, and to have tripled his expenses in order to accommodate Ellen's wish to travel with him, would have reduced the profit from the trip. As we have repeatedly seen, things are usually done Dickens's way or no way, so it would not be surprising if he had already decided not to take Ellen, and had entered into the pretence of making the assessment after he arrived so that it was the ever-loyal Wills who was left to break the bad news to Ellen.

So while the diary was greeted with great excitement and enthusiasm, and it clearly demonstrated the ongoing relationship between Dickens and Ellen, like everything else that has been presented in favour of the Wright/Storey narrative, it did not provide any evidence whatsoever as to the nature of the relationship.

While we are considering the American tour of 1867, it is worth looking at some of the thoughts expressed in the diary of Annie Fields at that time, which are described in George Curry's book *Charles Dickens and Annie Fields* (Huntington Library 1988).[38] Dickens's American publisher James Fields had visited Dickens in England in 1859, and it is clear they had become very great friends. Accordingly, Dickens stayed with the Fieldses at their home in Boston while on the 1867 tour. From her diaries, it is obvious that both James and Annie Fields were in thrall to their houseguest, Annie perhaps more so than James. However, there is no indication whatever to suggest that this impacted on the very deep love they held for each other – other than, if anything, increasing it. From the diaries it can be seen that both Annie and James very much enjoyed Dickens's company, and in his absence continued to hold him foremost in their thoughts. Annie, in particular, appeared to have suffered as much from Dickens's health problems as Dickens did himself. She also seemed to have been more upset than Dickens on the few occasions when she thought his audiences were not as appreciative of his performances as they should have been. Annie apparently kept a comprehensive diary in which she recorded some of her innermost thoughts, and after Dickens left America at the end of his tour, Annie continued to write of him in her diary. Not once did she mention the name of Ellen Ternan but understandably, Ellen is believed to be 'the beloved', an epithet she did use in her diary. The diaries still do not give any clear picture of the relationship between Dickens and Ellen. However, Ackroyd tells us that Mrs Fields was a highly respectable, and respected, Bostonian from a distinguished family, this being made quite clear in a later entry in her diary of that year when she condemns a man from her husband's firm who was found to have engaged in an adulterous relationship. Ackroyd also expressed the view that it is inconceivable that a woman who spoke in such terms about marital unfaithfulness would also have described in so glowing and rapturous a way Dickens's relationship with his 'beloved' – unless it were something quite different from a sexual affair. Ackroyd believes that she would not have written in this way unless she considered Dickens's relationship with Ellen Ternan to be above reproach.

I think a possible explanation is that Dickens *did* discuss Ellen with the Fieldses in the context of considering the possibility of bringing her to America. He would have explained his youthful indiscretion which resulted in the birth of Ellen, his neglect of both Mrs Ternan and of Ellen over the first eighteen years, and his ongoing attempts to make reparation and amends for those years of neglect. It was probably those discussions which led to Dickens writing to Wills with the message that it was not possible to proceed with the plan for Ellen to join him, and led Annie Fields to describe Ellen as Dickens's 'beloved' back in England. I further believe that this is why Annie Fields wrote in her diary immediately following Dickens's departure for England, 'May his mistakes be expiated'. Based on Ackroyd's opinion of Annie Fields, she would not be able to forgive his adultery, but by using the verb 'expiate' (make amends or reparation for wrongdoing) she could be sympathetic, knowing that he was actively trying to make amends. Thus, I believe that while being very cautious not to betray the confidences they had shared with Dickens during his stay with them, the words she uses in her diary do support the idea that the adultery was not an ongoing part of his life, but rather what we can see in Dickens's actions are his attempts to redress his earlier wrongdoing.

Having recovered from whatever the illnesses recorded in the 1867 diary were, and getting over the disappointment of not travelling to the United States, Ellen and her mother simply carried on as before until Dickens died.

It is important to mention here that Ellen's maid Jane Brown (neé Wheeler), who was in her service from 1866, apparently (according to Ackroyd) left a message for Ellen's daughter Gladys: 'if you had asked she would have told you the truth, your dear mother never was the mistress of Charles Dickens'.

Now this is not quite the same version as that reported by Slater in *The Great Charles Dickens Scandal*. Slater quotes a version, emanating from Ley, which ends with the same statement: 'never was the mistress of Charles Dickens'.[39] But later, he writes of the revelation by Katherine Longley that the statement by Jane Brown was in fact altered by Ley.[40] What Longley had discovered was that 'your dear mother never lived with Charles Dickens'.

So here there are various versions of the same story; 'mistress' or 'never lived with'. Given that the expression about an unmarried woman and a man 'living together' is usually a euphemism for them having a sexual relationship, there is probably no difference in meaning between the two versions, and they both make it clear that in the opinion of Ellen's maid and friend Jane, there was no sexual relationship between them, and by inference, no child. It is interesting to speculate why this very definite statement by Jane Brown does not receive the same recognition that the Wright and Storey statements do. In *The Invisible Woman*, Claire Tomalin mentions Jane Brown only in her being Ellen's maid and accompanying Ellen on her travels. Tomalin makes no mention at all of the message. Would it have something to do with the fact that Wright was a respected school teacher and was instrumental in the establishment of the Cowper Museum at Olney? And would it have something to do with Storey being the daughter of a Royal Academician who could name people such as Somerset Maugham and various Lords and Ladies of the Realm as personal friends? And would it have something to do with Jane Brown being only the humble maid of 'the greedy little gold-digging mistress'? Whatever reasons one might find to explain the difference, the most important reason of course is that Jane Brown's message directly contradicts the belief in the mistress version of the story, and therefore must be ignored.

So what can be made of the Wright/Storey narrative if Jane was telling the truth and had absolutely nothing to gain on her deathbed by lying? The next chapter will examine very closely what Wright and Storey actually did write.

Chapter Nine

Dismantling the Wright/Storey Story

Analysis is the Critical Starting Point of Strategic Thinking

Kenichi Ohmae

In this little volume I have asked the question, 'is there any explanation, other than the standard Wright/Storey narrative, for what we can see in the relationship between Charles Dickens and Ellen Ternan?' I think I have provided a reasoned alternative, that Ellen was his illegitimate daughter, and whether you agree with it or not is entirely up to you. I have been honest in stating that I have discovered no additional evidence beyond what is already in the public domain, and that what I have done is simply interpret that evidence as I see it, without relying on anyone else's opinions. I have certainly tried not to be influenced by second, third and even fourth-hand unsubstantiated hearsay and tittle-tattle, into which category I freely admit I put both Thomas Wright of Olney and Gladys Storey. But I must ask that question once again, if I am to be faithful to my research principles. And yes, I find there is still another explanation.

In his rather vicious attacks on the integrity and motives of Mrs Ternan and her daughter Ellen, Harrison makes statements such as 'the greedy little gold-digging mistress, always accompanied by her mama'. I am surprised that he did not actually turn those around to refer to 'his greedy gold-digging mistress, always accompanied by her daughter'. Apart from the assertion about their mercenary nature, much of what we see could well be interpreted to be either of those two relationships. Whether Dickens was Ellen's father or not, it is still possible that he started an affair with Mrs Ternan before she moved to Newcastle, which was rekindled in 1857. When Thackeray said 'no such thing, it's with an actress', the assumption was made that it was Ellen. But it could equally have been Mrs Ternan. Thackeray mentioned no name at all, so we cannot be sure who he actually thought it might have been. I am not going to pursue this any further since I believe that the weight of what we do know comes down more in favour of Mrs Ternan being the participant in an original affair resulting in Ellen being Dickens's daughter, than the affair with Mrs Ternan simply being rekindled. Under those circumstances, I don't think that Dickens would have gone to such lengths to provide for Ellen and for Mrs Ternan as appears to be the case. I mention it only because it is necessary to consider it, however briefly, as a possible alternative explanation.

Since I have suggested the possibility of Ellen being Dickens's daughter, we should look very closely at just how it might have come about, and I freely admit here that I am indulging myself and being very speculative. Over the years, the Ternans had travelled and acted widely across England, Ireland and America, but in June 1838 they were settled in London. Mrs Ternan was very popular and earning good money, but Mr Ternan was beginning to struggle, and only able to secure roles he considered to be beneath him. A review of his last performance, as Macbeth, in London prior to taking an engagement for a season in Newcastle, was very far from flattering:

> Mr Ternan's face, voice, figure and gait are all unsuited to the noble Thane. He gave the text correctly with tolerably good emphasis, but throughout the entire of his performance, there is nothing that we could discover, above the common place style of acting. We certainly expected more from Mr Ternan after his clever acting in Shylock and Iago. But as we have before said, the part is unsuited to him, he never can succeed in it. The part of Lady Macbeth was attempted by Mrs Lovell, it was a very sad exhibition. We never saw a play worse got up, there was scarcely a scene introduced that was in keeping with the piece, and from first to last the greatest pains appeared to have been bestowed to render this splendid play of our immortal bard's as unprofitable as possible. (From the *Court Gazette and Fashionable Guide*, Saturday, 23 June 1838)

Mrs Ternan's last performances in London were to be through June. And while her reviews were unanimously positive, with such a poor review of Mr Ternan's final London performance it would not have been surprising had Mrs Ternan felt some trepidation at yet another upheaval, especially with a couple of very young children. Acting had always been something of a precarious living, and embarking on a major, and uncertain change, especially as she personally was doing very well in London, might have caused her some anxiety. Further, she might well have been noticing the changes in Mr Ternan's personality and behaviour which eventually deteriorated to the extent that he would be incarcerated in the asylum.

In 1844, when Ellen was 5 years old, and a short while after his infant son Thomas had died, Mr Ternan had a mental breakdown of some sort, and was committed to the Bethnal Green asylum for the insane. There was no cure available in those days, and in order to protect other inmates, restraint was the only course available. This went as far as patients being chained to the walls in the early stages of illness, though as it took its course and the affected patient began to lose strength and mobility, this became unnecessary. Patients would become emaciated, incontinent and unable to feed themselves. They would be very susceptible to respiratory and other infections and die a rather miserable, painful and undignified death. Mr Ternan died in 1846.

General Paralysis of the Insane, also known as General Paresis, was identified as a specific disease in the early nineteenth century, and was originally considered to be a type of madness due to a dissolute character. It was not associated with syphilis until the late 1880s, well after the death of Thomas Ternan, so it is no surprise that syphilis is not mentioned in the Cause of Death certificate. If syphilis was indeed the cause of his incarceration and death as Claire Tomalin has understandably suggested, given the usual trajectory of the disease he probably picked up the infection some twenty to twenty-five years earlier, say around 1820 to 1825. He married Frances Jarman in 1834 and by then would have been well into the latent stage of the disease and no longer infectious. Accordingly, Mrs Ternan and her children would not have been at any risk of infection, but for Mr Ternan, the disease would have continued its progression towards the tertiary and final stage – death. His behaviour would have been changing; for a few years prior to his admission to the asylum, he would have been increasingly difficult to live with. Macready noted in his diary:

> I do not like Ternan's mode of behaviour: it is difficult to say who will or will not be an actor, but I do not think this person in his private capacity will ever shed lustre on the theatrical profession. He seems to me opinionated, jealous and of course little-minded.

So this is the situation in which Mrs Ternan found herself in June 1838. There is no indication whether she was aware, or even suspected, that her husband had possibly contracted syphilis earlier in his life before they were married, or whether she was blissfully ignorant. But even had she known, neither she nor Mr Ternan would have been aware of what was coming; as mentioned, the link between general paralysis of the insane and syphilis was not made until well beyond his death. But she surely would have noticed the changes creeping into her husband's behaviour that led eventually to his admission to the Bethnal Green asylum in 1844, whether they were caused by syphilis or not. She might have confided in her friend William Macready; after all, it was Macready who stood her friend and provided some financial assistance immediately following her husband's death. Macready was also a great friend of Charles Dickens, and it is not inconceivable that Dickens had met Mrs Ternan through that friendship.

Dickens would have been aware of the Ternans impending departure from London, and might well have gone to the theatre while Catherine was away at Twickenham recovering from the birth of Mary, to see one last performance and to wish Mrs Ternan well in her new venture. As she was about to leave the place at which she had been made welcome, felt secure and very successful, it would be natural for her to express some sadness, even if not concern, at the prospect before her. A few tears, a sympathetic ear, a comforting hug, and Mrs Ternan leaves for Newcastle carrying a microscopically small Ellen in utero. Dickens returns to work with a microscopically small skeleton in his closet. Pure speculation! But by no means impossible. What one might now call 'a one-night-stand', or perhaps, 'a youthful indiscretion'.

The skeleton continued to grow from 'those days you remember when Mary was born', through to the point where Dickens eventually needed to deal with it, which is exactly what he did in 1857/58. And of course, he did it his way.

But we still need to explain, if we can, how Gladys Storey came to the conclusion that 'there was a boy but it died'. Let us return to where the story of the baby all started, and look very closely at what she wrote in *Dickens and Daughter*. There is so very little of it that I think we can be generous with our time to examine all of what there is.

Dickens and Daughter purports to tell the true story of the relationship between Dickens and his younger daughter Katey (Perugini). It comprises some 230 pages of gossip gleaned mostly from Katey during afternoon teas and fireside chats at which either Gladys Storey or her mother, and frequently both, were present. It is for the most part very detailed; for example there are ten pages devoted to Dickens's attempts to cure by hypnosis the wife of an unnamed friend, who had some sort of mental health problem; it details a party which started at 3.30 pm and continued until 6.30 pm; it detailed the estate of Georgina Hogarth as valued (very precisely stated by Storey) at £317 6s.3d.; and that of Henry Dickens as £1,803 6s 6d. But when it comes to Ellen Ternan and her child there is but one short sentence. And as for the rest of the Ellen/Dickens relationship, that is comprised within seven scattered sentences. As there is so very little, and the book itself a bit difficult to get one's hands on, I shall reproduce, almost verbatim, all that there is, in the sequence in which it is presented to us.

The first mention of Ellen appears on page 90, simply included in the cast list for the Manchester performances of *The Frozen Deep*. And then, on page 91 Storey tells us: 'It is known only to a few that Mrs Perugini wrote a life of her father.'

Apparently, Katey then burnt the manuscript because she believed she had told only half of the truth, and was concerned that if it was made public in that state, readers would not get the whole truth, and would get the facts all wrong. So, according to Gladys Storey, Katey asked her to write the unvarnished truth – as Katey would give it to her.

Those few lines are on page 91, and present Storey's justification for the book: to tell the 'whole truth'. Then, on page 93, there is a short paragraph:

There is no doubt that the children of his imagination came before his children of the flesh, [this in Storey's voice, and therefore probably her opinion rather than

Katey's], which may have accounted for Mrs Perugini saying: 'The only fault I found with my father was that he had too many children', a remark far-reaching in its depth of meaning.

Why Storey should consider the remark 'far-reaching', we shall never know. If she was referring to the baby who died, the poor little chap could not have reached very far. If he was born in 1862 (or later), Dickens and Catherine had already separated by then, so he could not have been the cause of that trouble.

In reading this piece, we should bear in mind that Ellen was not only a child of his flesh, she was, in my interpretation, for eighteen years a very important figure living in his imagination. He had no alternative other than to imagine her growing up and her development, and as I have pointed out, she frequently made her presence felt in his novels and short stories.

There then follows a brief description, amounting to two pages, of Dickens's physical appearance and mental attributes, before Storey actually mentions Ellen, describing her as small, fair-haired and rather pretty and, coming into Dickens's life, enslaved him. Storey goes on to mention Mrs Winter (née Beadnell) writing to Dickens, and then quotes from Dickens's letter to Forster that I have already mentioned, although she does not acknowledge Forster as the source: 'His observation regarding his wife at this time, that it was a pity he "ever fell in her way" was subsequently to become the retributory thought of this girl regarding herself and Dickens when (after his death) she married a clergyman and became the mother of his children.'

This is in Storey's voice, and other than a bias against Ellen, already indicated in the previous extract suggesting that it was all Ellen's fault, I am unsure as to how Storey can put that 'retributory thought' into her head; I doubt very much that Ellen told her or Katey that she regretted her association with Dickens when she married Wharton Robinson.

This is followed immediately by the *only* mention, entirely in Storey's voice, of a child: 'More tragic and far-reaching in its effects was the association of Charles Dickens and Ellen Ternan and their resultant son (who died in infancy), than that of Nelson and Lady Hamilton and their daughter.'

As this single sentence is the sole foundation on which the whole saga of Dickens's fathering a child with Ellen is based, with not a shred of evidence to support it, I think it is essential to try to make some sense, if at all possible, of this comparison with Nelson, his mistress Lady Hamilton, and their illegitimate child.

The story of Nelson and Lady Hamilton is too long to describe in detail here. Suffice to say, Lady Emma Hamilton was a married woman at the time of Nelson's taking her, very openly, as a mistress, and together they had a daughter, Horatia. Not surprisingly, a result of the affair was that Mrs Nelson left her husband. Horatia thrived, and eventually married a clergyman, giving birth to ten children of her own. By contrast, the situation as described by Storey is that Dickens took a young unmarried woman as his mistress, secretively, and together they had a son who died. Catherine Dickens had already left the family home prior to this happening, so that could not be included as one of the 'far reaching effects'. Thus, in no way could Dickens's relationship with Ellen at this time be described as being 'more tragic and far-reaching in its effects' than Nelson's actions. On the other hand, if one keeps an open mind and considers the possibility of Dickens having fathered a child with Mrs Ternan some eighteen years earlier, you do get a version that is at least a shadow of the Nelson/Hamilton affair. In this alternative version Dickens had an affair with a married woman (Mrs Ternan) and they did have a daughter (Ellen) who thrived. Catherine Dickens did leave him partly because of the affair, and the daughter, Ellen, went on to marry a clergyman and had two children. As I said, a shadow of Nelson's affair by comparison, but at least a comparable reflection of the Nelson–Lady Hamilton situation. I would even go so far as to suggest that this is the whole story that Katey wanted to be told, but just like Thomas Wright, Storey got hold of the wrong end of the stick and 'got it all wrong', as Katey had feared.

This is followed a couple of pages later by an anecdote of Catherine's tears at being asked by Dickens to meet Ellen. This is clearly before Dickens and Catherine had actually separated. Storey tells us that discovering her mother in tears, Katey asked her why she was upset. Storey goes on to relate that Catherine had apparently been asked by Dickens to visit Ellen. Storey then continues with the statement that early in their married life Dickens and Catherine had made a compact that if either of them fell in love with anybody else, they were to tell one another. Storey believed that Dickens remembered that compact, and had asked Catherine to call upon the girl with whom he had fallen in love.

It is unclear where Storey found the statement about the pact between Dickens and Catherine; presumably we are to accept that it was from Katey. But, within five lines of that anecdote, Storey already writes a very significant variation of what Katey is supposed to have said. Storey's original version was 'Dickens had *asked* Catherine to go and see Ellen Ternan.' Storeys variation, just a few lines later was 'Dickens had *told* his wife to call upon the girl with whom he had fallen in love.'

Originally 'asked', now 'told', and no previous mention of Dickens having fallen in love with Ellen. Storey is clearly distorting the truth quite considerably by making these two very small but significant changes. In the original version we are given no reason for the request for Catherine to visit Ellen. It might have been 'because she's my mistress', but it could equally well have been 'because she is my daughter'. I cannot imagine Dickens being so cruel as to ask Catherine to visit his mistress; nobody would gain anything from that, and it would have been as distressing for Ellen as it would have been for Catherine, which Dickens surely would not have wanted. But I can imagine him asking her to visit his illegitimate child, hoping for some conciliation and her acceptance of the situation, for Ellen's sake. If she was his daughter, that would make her a half-sister to their other children, and maybe he was also hoping for some acceptance of Ellen into the family circle. It is also strange that there was absolutely no follow-up information as to how well or badly the meeting went. It seems that Catherine did make the visit – if Storey is to be believed – so having mentioned it, one might have expected some idea as to the outcome, if one is telling the whole truth. It is interesting to note that just as Storey changed 'asked' to 'told', so Claire Tomalin in *The Invisible Woman* went further and used the word 'ordered'. And then Lucinda Hawksley, in her book *Katie*[41] retains Tomalin's 'ordered', but then goes even further and adds, 'but Charles could be a tartar and Catherine was bullied into it'. Michael Slater later uses an older form of command, and writes that 'she prepared to go at Dickens's behest and make a courtesy call on Ellen'. Katie's original 'asked' was quite clear and unambiguous and did not need to be changed in any way. However, it has been, and one can only surmise that each of the later commentators changed it for no purpose other than making Dickens appear to be more dictatorial and cruel than he actually was. There are other versions of the anecdote, including Catherine being asked to visit Mrs Ternan (rather than Ellen), and asking Catherine to invite the Ternans to Tavistock house, rather than visiting them. Messy, but actually telling us nothing about the nature of the relationship!

In the Storey account, there is absolutely no indication as to when and where the child was born, nor when, how, where or why it died. There is no indication as to when and how Katey learned of the baby; no mention of Ellen's long and lonely ordeal and Dickens's mysterious disappearances to France through 1862/3; no mention of any problems involving Ellen being ill and Wills being called to Slough in 1867. The problem here is that of different chronologies: the chronology of when events occurred, and the chronology of when information about the events came into the public domain. Storey is unlikely to have been aware of Dickens's correspondence which mentioned Ellen's ordeal in 1862, and could not have known of the lost diary of 1867 as it was not found and examined until the 1940s – *after* Storey's account was published.

Katey apparently mentioned no date at all, which is strange, to say the least. Did Katey actually *know* about the child, or did she simply *believe* it to have been born and died? We can't be sure. Is it likely that Katey could have actually known about a birth and death, and tell Gladys Storey about it without also knowing at least the year in which it is supposed to have happened? Is it possible that Katey was fully aware of the real truth, but preferred to believe (and told Storey) that her father had had an affair later in his life, than to accept that she had an illegitimate half-sister? It seems to me that while Mary was quite close to Ellen, and had welcomed her to Gad's Hill, Katey was much more reticent about her.

We shall never really know how it all came about, but suppose that Dickens had remembered that compact much earlier, say at the time when Mary was born, and had told Catherine then about his youthful indiscretion with Mrs Ternan in 1838? In an earlier chapter I have suggested that Catherine might have been aware of, or perhaps held suspicions about, Ellen, which would have been difficult for her to live with. In the lead up to their separation, during the family discussions resulting in 'everyone being made aware of the situation', as claimed by Dickens in his 'Violated Letter' and restated by Katey (see below), suppose someone – either Dickens himself or perhaps Catherine (the only two in the family who would have known) – mentions an actress and a child, and of course the family members present would want to know: Who? When? Where is it? Etc. The simple answer of 'there was a boy but he died' would be a very clever response to such questions. If this is how Katey learnt of the baby that died, and there is no indication of her learning at any other time, it could not possibly have been born to Ellen. Stating it to be a boy would deflect any suspicion away from Ellen being the child, and claiming it to have died would certainly put an end to any further questions. Storey then gets half the truth from Katey during the fireside chats, assumes that Ellen is the actress being referred to, and then promulgates the untruth of Ellen being the mother of Dickens's child, rather than the most probable alternative version, that she *was* the child.

Gladys Storey then goes on to report that as far as Catherine, the elder children, Georgina Hogarth and John Forster were concerned, 'all was open' regarding the affair – he concealed nothing. It was his wish that things should be that way.

Storey describes some readings given by Dickens, and inter alia slots in a sentence telling us that a settlement was made on Ellen, who subsequently lived in a house of her own at Peckham. But Michael Slater points out this was not so, and surmises that Katey had 'telescoped certain events in her memory'. She had either forgotten, or perhaps never knew, that Ellen had her own house in Mornington Crescent, and had subsequently lived with her mother in Slough before moving to Nunhead (which is near Peckham) in 1867. There is no further mention of Ellen until page 128. Dickens by now had settled at Gad's Hill, and Storey tells us that in April 1869 Ellen Ternan came to stay there. Storey gives no indication as to how long the visit lasted, or who else might have been present, but apparently they played cricket. When Katey heard of Ellen's earlier visit and that she had taken a hand at cricket, according to Storey she said, 'I am afraid that she did not play the game!'

I think it has been made quite clear from other accounts that following Dickens's death, Mary and Georgina both made Ellen welcome at Gad's Hill. It is not unknown in such cases for one or more half-siblings and other 'step-relatives' to be welcoming toward the illegitimate member, while others in the family are less so. In light of that, I do not think one can attach much significant meaning to Katey's statement about Ellen 'not playing the game'.

And now you have the sum total of what Gladys Storey wrote about Ellen in her book *Dickens and Daughter*, which was written in order to fulfil the promise she made to Katey to tell the whole unvarnished truth. If I were Katey Perugini, I think I would have been very disappointed in the result. In the manuscript which Katey destroyed because it told only 'half the truth', we have no idea of what constituted that 'half-truth'. But if Storey has given the world the whole truth, the manuscript that Katey burnt must have been a very small volume indeed!

It seems to me that Storey's version must be far less even than half the truth, and that Katey had chosen her amanuensis very badly. To me it appears that Storey and her mother simply hoovered up any little tittle-tattle they heard, and pocketed any little knick-knack Katey chose to toss their way, over several years of afternoon teas and fireside chats. However, it must be noted that at many of those little chats, there were also other guests present, and it is unlikely that Katey would have been very open on those occasions. So, over the time, maybe Katey did not manage to convey the whole truth, and when Gladys Storey came to write it all down over the ensuing ten years, she was completely unable to put it into any sensible narrative because she and her mother had gleaned only half, or less, of the story. While they then had time to do a little research to fill in the incredible detail which appears in some of the anecdotes, detail probably not gathered directly from Katey (such as the precise value of the various deceased estates referred to), they were unable to check any details of the putative birth. By the time they considered it ready for publication Katey had been dead for a decade, and could not confirm whether what Storey had written really was what she had wanted the public to know.

Before leaving Gladys Storey, I think it is relevant to mention that there are two other babies who come into the category of a 'son (who died in infancy)', one definitely related to Ellen. I am referring of course to her brother Thomas Ternan, born in 1842 and who failed to thrive and died. If, as I have suggested, there was some talk in the lead up to his separation from Catherine, of some indiscretion on Dickens's part, then with a conflation of pregnancies and slippage of time, it is not beyond the realms of possibility that it was this baby Ternan who became 'the resultant son (who died in infancy)'. It is quite clear that Dickens could not have been the father of baby Thomas because, while he was on his way to Scotland with Catherine at the time of Thomas's conception, the route they took did not go anywhere near Newcastle. But given all the other confusions and the absence of detail about the birth and death of the putative baby, it is worth considering the death of baby Ternan for the sake of completeness.

The other baby who failed to thrive, and comes within the same category, is baby Perugini, Katie's own son. Again, Katie reminiscing over her own loss, but being misunderstood by the Storeys, could well result in them thinking that it was Ellen's baby that Katie was talking about. Of course, I have no evidence, but – I must point out – neither does anyone else. As it is, Storey's book is so lacking in detail with respect to Ellen and a child, but so chock-full of detail about the sayings and doings of the rich and famous persons who visited Katey in her final years, it is surprising that anyone could take it seriously.

Thomas Wright's statements about Ellen being Dickens's mistress were published some four years prior to Storey's book, but Storey makes no mention of them at all. She apparently claimed to have been unaware of Wright's books at the time of writing hers, which is possible, but, I think, unlikely. According to Wright, Ellen had disburdened her soul to the Reverend Benham, and had told him 'the whole story'. That version of the story, supposedly from Ellen's own lips according to Wright, made no mention whatsoever of a child. On the other hand, Katey's version from her own lips, according to Storey, did include a child. Which of the two women is most likely to have known, and told, the truth? Had there been a child, Ellen would have experienced it, and therefore would have *known*. But Katey could only have heard about it, and probably *believed* it to be true. Thus, Wright's version in relation to a baby is more likely to be correct. But I still doubt Wright's account of Ellen being Dickens's mistress. I am firmly of the belief that Wright had simply picked up on the rumours that had circulated at the time of the Dickenses' separation and had believed them to be true. Whatever Ellen had said to Benham, and however it then came across to Wright, Wright would have been predisposed to believe the mistress view. Wright would have been aware of the 'Violated Letter' and of Dickens's 'Personal Statement' and would have certainly been aware that 'something was going on'.

While Wright made no mention in his books about a 'baby boy that died', it is important to note that Katharine Longley has uncovered some notes written by Wright which indicates 'there were children'. It appears that Wright had claimed this in a letter he had written to *The Observer* on 15 November 1935, but which was rejected and never published. It seems, according to Longley, that while Wright stated the name of his informant to be a Rev. George A. Payne, that was not in fact the case. Longley states that a Mrs Thorncroft met with Wright in December 1834 and had mentioned to him then that Dickens had had a 'natural son'. Mrs Thorncroft said that she had received the information 'from an aged aunt, who had got it from another person'. Mrs Thorncroft then added that the other person was a Unitarian minister who had just died. As with many of these claims, it has been very difficult to get at the truth for the simple reason that many of the so-called 'informants' seem to have died before their revelations were set free in the public domain. Maybe Wright did not mention this in his books, because even he thought that a story involving an aged aunt and a deceased vicar would not have a great deal of credibility.

Longley pursued her investigations and eventually wrote a mammoth tome entitled *A Pardoner's Tale: Charles Dickens and the Ternan Family*, which is a strident defence of Ellen's character. Being some 300,000 words long, it was never published, but Michael Slater comments that the title itself indicates that it had 'a fatal flaw, namely, the existence in the researcher's mind of a foregone conclusion'. I believe that many commentaries on the Dickens/Ellen relationship suffer that same defect.

So if there was no child born to Ellen, why did Storey write that it was? When questioned she said, 'All is based in truth'. It may have been based in truth, it is just that the half-truths she gleaned have been put together into a monstrous untruth.

According to Storey, Katey feared for the truth to come out, 'lest those who revealed it – not being in possession of the true facts – would get them all wrong'. It seems to me that Storey did an excellent job of realising Katey's fears.

Chapter Ten

Other Odds and Sods of 'Evidence'

All that glisters is not gold.
William Shakespeare *The Merchant of Venice*

There are many anecdotes spread through various biographies of Charles Dickens and Ellen Ternan which contribute very little to our understanding of the relationship between the two. Some of them are undated, and some are only reports of hearsay, but since they do frequently appear, albeit as different versions, and generally stressed so as to give support to the standard narrative, I think they should be included here. You might think I am being too pernickety about very few words, but in reality those very few words, reporting and interpreting what little we actually know, are all we have. Accordingly, I think they do indeed deserve very close scrutiny, particularly in the total absence of any substantial evidence.

As previously mentioned, on the Tuesday following the Manchester performances of *The Frozen Deep* and *Uncle John*, the Ternans were engaged to play at Doncaster, and Dickens and Wilkie Collins contrived to visit them there. According to Claire Tomalin(*Invisible Woman*) 'At some point Dickens *elicited* the information he wanted about the Ternans' next engagement [my italics]', and in her biography of Dickens, that is restated as ... Dickens had *found out* that Mrs Ternan and her three daughters were going to be in Doncaster [my italics].'

According to Lucinda Hawksley, 'On the way back to London, *in full view of Catherine and Georgina,* Charles *innocently* enquired of Mrs Ternan where the family would be performing next; she told him they were engaged to appear in Doncaster [my italics].'

The embellishment of these sentences with words such as 'elicited', 'found out', 'in full view' and 'innocently', indicates to me a wish to make it look as though Dickens was being underhand in determining where they were going, and he was also being very insensitive, even cruel, to Catherine. By contrast, Ackroyd simply says 'Dickens *had heard* that the Ternans were about to travel to the North, to appear in a special season at Doncaster [my italics].'

I think it very likely that even when he was booking Mrs Ternan and her daughters for *The Frozen Deep*, they would have consulted their diaries to make sure they were free to accept, and would have mentioned to him their following gig at Doncaster.

The next anecdote concerns Dickens and Ellen being spotted out walking. In *The Invisible Woman*, Claire Tomalin refers to an undated letter written to an unnamed addressee by Thackeray's daughter Anny, in which she says she 'has heard that Charley met his father & Miss whatever the actress' name out walking on Hampstead Heath'. Anny goes on to say that she 'didn't believe a word of the scandal'.

Tomalin then mentions a formal letter to his elder children accusing their mother of not having the character to appreciate his platonic attachment to Nelly, but does not quote directly from it, nor does she give a specific date. But Tomalin might be referring to a letter mentioned by Lucinda Hawksley (a great-great-great-granddaughter of Dickens) in her book *Katey*. In that book Hawksley writes: 'Dickens was infatuated enough to risk being seen out in public on his own with Ellen. He was observed wandering romantically across Hampstead Heath with Ellen on his arm; the person who spotted them was his own son Charley.' Hawksley goes on to say that during the first half of 1858 Charles wrote a letter to his children, apparently informing them that he would not tolerate any innuendo about Ellen. The letter goes on to say that she was chaste and virtuous, that he was beyond reproach and that it was Catherine who refused to understand the simple beauty of his relationship with the actress. Hawksley then tells us that the letter has not survived the ravages of family editing. Of course, 'the simple beauty' of his relationship could well have been a very normal, loving, father/daughter relationship and the claim that Dickens was 'infatuated enough to risk being seen' then becomes a nonsense.

It is unclear whether Lucinda Hawksley had actually seen this letter prior to its demise at the hands of the family editors, or whether it has become an oral tradition within the family. Whatever the case, Michael Slater (*The Great Charles Dickens Scandal*) tells it again slightly differently. Slater's version is:

> as can be seen from a letter written to a friend (still unnamed) by Thackeray's daughter Annie, later Lady Ritchie, in late December 1858: 'Papa says the story is that Charley (Dickens's eldest son, aged twenty-one)

met his father & Miss Whatsname Whatever the actress out walking on Hampstead Heath.

Now here we do have a date, late December 1858, which would be well after the 'first half of 1858' when the letter supposedly sent to his children was written. Of course I realise that all of this occurred some 160 years ago, and it is to be expected that times might slip and become rather unreliable and imprecise. But it does mean that extra vigilance is required when drawing conclusions from vague sources.

Another anecdote from about this time is that of the trinket that mistakenly found its way into Catherine's hands. (I mentioned this in an earlier chapter in relation to Dickens attending a performance of *Faust* in Paris). There are at least five iterations of this anecdote to be found. Lucinda Hawksley's version is: 'Charles had ordered a gold bracelet and, assuming quite naturally that it was for his client's wife, the jeweller delivered it to Catherine. It had been intended for Ellen.'

However, Michael Slater reports on a more embellished version. According to Slater, the painter Elisabeth Jerichau-Baumann wrote from London to Hans Christian Anderson in Denmark:

> D. had sent a bracelet with a poem to an actress; it got lost, and D. advertised for it in the papers. It was sent, his wife received it, thinking it was a present for her; she put it on, the poem fell out – and she never forgave him that after having been married to her for 25 years he could enter into an understanding with another.

Slater also included the following version of the same anecdote as it was reprinted in the *Detroit Free Press*, 22 June, 1858:

> I hear that Dickens has for some time been paying attention to an actress at the Haymarket (Amy Sedgwick, it is thought). So charmed was he that he went to Hunt and Roskell's and bought her a beautiful bracelet ... and had the lady's name engraved upon it. The trinket was unfortunately lost one night when he was taking her to a place of amusement and was found by some honest person, who took it to Hunt and Roskell's, who at once sent it to Mr Dickens, and as Mr Dickens was out, Mrs Dickens received the naughty tell-tale. She presented it to her lord when he came home, and simply said 'Charles I wish you would not be so open in these matters', whereupon ... the editor of Household Words went into a towering passion, and said he would not stay another minute in the same house with his wife.

Another version, as reported by Slater, refers to the trinket anecdote as: 'Dickens having presented a brooch or bracelet with his portrait to Miss Sedgwick or some other actress.' The anecdote continues in similar vein as the previous version but concludes with: 'Mrs Dickens had her suspicions, no doubt that all was not as it should be, and went with her daughter to the theatre where, on the appearance of the said actress, the brooch or bracelet was seen upon her.'

Yet another variation claims that it was Georgina who had spilt the beans and given the game away! The last version I shall include here is that:

Catherine visited the jeweller to make a purchase of her own, and was surprised when the assistant asked how she liked her new bracelet. The discovery that Dickens had recently ordered such an item clearly not intended for herself 'opened her eyes' about his relationship with Ellen and a separation speedily followed.

All these versions of the trinket tell us very little other than there was, at the time, confusion as to the identity of the actress involved, and that over the years the various commentators have definitely settled on its being Ellen. But they still provide no clue as to the relationship that existed then, or later in the decade prior to Dickens's death.

I now want to turn to a few letters written by Dickens following the Manchester performances, which ran from 20 August to 25 August. The particular letters were spread rather thinly between 28 August 1857 and 23 January 1858, and largely refer to his state of mind at this time. Some, such as the 'riddle' letters to Wills, and the 'what is befalling me now' letter to Forster, have already been mentioned and I will not detail them again here. But there are several letters to different people in which Dickens writes of his 'excess energy', of 'scaling all the peaks in Switzerland', and of 'conquering ogres', all indicating a certain level of irrationality in his mind. But we have seen these sentiments expressed before. For example, in the so-called 'joke' letters to his friends at the time of Queen Victoria's marriage he wrote 'of running away to some uninhabited island with a maid of honour', and in the letter to Forster in 1854 he wrote of having thoughts of running to the Pyrenees Mountains. There is no doubt that even at those times Dickens was troubled in his marriage to Catherine, and in late

1857, it was becoming much, much worse. He has just come down from an incredible 'high' with first the organisation and management of the Jerrold fundraising, then the performances, then the accusation by Douglas Jerrold's son of bringing his father's character into question by putting it around that his widow was in need of charity. That seemed to upset Dickens a lot, and to add to it all he was trying to deal with his conscience about Ellen and Mrs Ternan. His plans to make reparation for his earlier wrongdoings were thrown into chaos by Mrs Hogarth's scurrilous accusation about his relationship with Georgina, rapidly followed by the accusation of his having an affair with an actress. It is no wonder that his letters were sometimes indicative of irrationality, but they in no way add anything to our understanding of his relationship to Ellen. Despite their being included in many of the biographies of Dickens, we can learn no more from them than can be learnt from the 'Violated Letter' and his 'Personal Statement'.

I will mention here one more source – which is little more than gossip, but has been included in some, though not all, biographies of Dickens. This comes from the pen of the writer Mrs Elizabeth Lynn Linton, who died in 1898, and whose memoir[42] was published posthumously a year later. A Mr W. Robertson Nicoll informs us that:

> These papers were written for a periodical at my request. The authoress proposed to make them a fairly complete chronicle of her literary life, but did not live to finish them. It has been thought, however, that the sketches she was able to write possess an independent value which justifies republication.

An introduction by Beatrice Harraden to the memoir, reads:

> It is to be regretted that she did not begin this task earlier in her old age: we might then have had a complete picture of the times in which she lived, instead of these desultory fragments, which are of necessity merely a harbinger of what she really knew and had seen. It is to be regretted also that she is not here herself to tone down some of her more pungent remarks and criticisms, hastily thrown off in bitter moments such as come to us all. Mrs Linton's pen was ever harsher than her speech, and those who loved and knew her have the right to emphasize this fact – even in a preface.

Mrs Lynn Linton first met Dickens at a dinner hosted by Walter Savage Landor, the guests including herself, Forster and Dickens. Later she became a contributor to *Household Words* and a friend of Wills. In *The Invisible Woman*, Clare Tomalin writes:

> Ellen ... was certainly aware of the remarks of Mrs Lynn Linton in her memoirs, in which she referred to Dickens's secret history, his mad, passionate love and the way in which he was deceived, tricked and betrayed by one he never suspected or found out. .... Nelly – it's hard to see who else she can have meant – was caught in a web of deceit. ... vague as they are, Mrs Lynn Linton's are the most damaging remarks ..... because they are the only ones that contain the accusation of trickery by Nelly.

Two points immediately spring to mind reading this short extract. First, Tomalin has attached Ellen's name (Nelly) not based on any evidence, but simply because 'it's hard to see who else she can have meant'. And having made that assumption, elevates the importance of the statements, 'because they are the only ones that contain the accusation of trickery by Nelly'.

There are other, less immediately obvious, problems with this extract, which include the variations that Tomalin has made to Linton's original memoir. First, the reference to 'secret history' actually reads in the Lynn Linton memoir:

> Dickens had no eye for beauty, per se. He could love a comparatively plain woman – and did; but Thackeray's fancy went out to loveliness; and cleverness alone, without beauty – which ruled Dickens – would never have stirred his passions. Both men could, and did, love deeply, passionately, madly, and the secret history of their lives has yet to be written.

This comes from a comparison Lynn Linton is making between Dickens and Thackeray, and applies to *both* men. And further, Tomalin's version of the sentence, seemingly referring only to Dickens, goes on to refer to Dickens being 'deceived and tricked', which is an idea which does not form part of Lynn Linton's original sentence. That observation is found several pages later in the memoir, again, still in a comparison with Thackeray:

> How bright he was! How keen and observant! His eyes seemed to penetrate through yours into your very brain,

and he was one of the men to whom, had I been given that way, I could not have dared to tell a lie. He would have seen the truth written in plain characters behind the eyes, and traced in the lines about the mouth. His look was of the kind which *dévalisés* the mind; and straight as he was in his own character, he would have caught the crookedness of another as by the consciousness of contrasts. And yet I know one cleverer, more astute, less straight than himself, who sailed round him and deceived him from start to finish; who tricked and betrayed him, and was never suspected nor found out.

The spatial distribution within the memoir of the separate subjects of love and of deception shows that there is no real justification for putting them sequentially into the same sentence, and then drawing the single conclusion that Ellen was both the object of his love, and his deceiver. So, if not Ellen, who was the 'plain woman', the object of his love, and who was the deceiver?

While we are looking at extracts from Mrs Lynn Linton's memoir, which, it must be remembered, is a memoir of *her* literary life, not a biography of either Dickens or of Thackeray, let us look at what she had to say of John Forster following that initial dinner with Landor:

Forster was saturnine and cynical. He was the 'harbitary gent' of the cabman's rank, and one of the most jealous of men. Dickens and Landor were his property – pocket-boroughs in a way – and he resented the introduction of a third person and a stranger. He carried his spite so far as not to include in his collected works a very beautiful little poem which Mr Landor had written to me, and which – never mind the subject of the verse – merited a prominent place for its intrinsic beauty. He was as treacherous, too, and disloyal as he was egotistic and jealous; and I had the satisfaction of reviewing his Life of Landor, when, as poor Shirley Brooks said to Monckton Milnes, suiting the action to the word, I took the skin off him. I thought this Life a disgraceful thing for a friend to have written, for Mr Landor believed in Forster – made him his literary executor, and gave him all the proceeds of his works, and used to call him 'Good Forster'. When he was dead and done with, and of no more value to the man he had trusted, then the true nature of the 'friendship' came to light, and the result was a cold and carping and unsympathetic biography, which I for one did my best to show in its true colours.

Quite clearly Mrs Lynn Linton was no fan of John Forster, and this account of his relationship with Landor is certainly seasoned with the flavour of deceit. And if she found that Landor had been deceived, tricked and betrayed to such an extent by Forster, it is most likely that it was also he who was in her sights when writing of Dickens being deceived. If so, the object of Dickens's love must have been another person altogether. For an answer let us look at a letter written by Katey Perugini some six years after publication of Mrs Lynn Linton's memoir. Katey wrote to her friend Anne, Lady Ritchie (Thackeray's eldest daughter), quoted here from *Katey* by

Lucinda Hawksley: 'I am amused and irritated by Mrs Lyne Lynton (sic). How did she know who were our father's loves? Of this I am certain; that neither of them ever loved *her*, and what she says of *my* father seemed to imply that he did!'

In the footnote to this extract of the letter, Hawksley says of Mrs Lynn Linton: 'Her writings about Charles in the memoirs were veiled but darkly hinted at scandal, guaranteed to get gossipy tongues speculating as to what she had intended.'

As is often the way, opinions and observations such as these by contemporaries of the subject of biographies are frequently posthumous publications, giving no one any opportunity to question the author as to quite what they did mean. Unlike Claire Tomalin, Lucinda Hawksley makes no attempt to interpret either Linton's memoir or Katey's letter, but clearly Katey was of the opinion that in writing about Dickens's passionate love, Mrs Lynn Linton was possibly thinking of herself being the 'plain woman' loved by Dickens.

As an aside, Mrs Lynton wrote in her memoir:

> I did not know either man intimately; but if not the rose itself, I knew those who stood near. Their close friends were also mine, and I heard more than I saw. Many secret confidences were passed on to me, which, of course, I have kept sacred; and both men would have been surprised had they known how much I knew of things uncatalogued and unpublished. This consciousness of unsuspected participation gives a strange sense of secret intimacy, which adds a curious piquancy to the outward formalities de rigueur between those who are personally unfamiliar.

This is in contrast to a statement made by Thomas Wright in his biography of Dickens in which he claims that Dickens and Mrs Lynn Linton were intimate and remained excellent friends long after he had purchased Gads Hill from her.

While on the subject of Thomas Wright and his use of the word 'intimate' in relation to Dickens and Mrs Lynn Linton, it is appropriate to go back to Wright's statement about Ellen loathing the thought of intimacy with Dickens. Wright claimed that these were Benham's words, but Wright himself uses 'intimate' and its derivative 'intimacy' liberally through his biography of Dickens. Other biographers have done the same. In not one of them is it used to denote a sexual relationship. Rather it is simply used to describe very close relationships between people. A few examples from Wright include:

Preface, page 5: 'Dickens's intimate friends, Percy Fitzgerald and John Hollingshead.'

Page 56: 'The dramatic critic of the True Sun was John Forster, who became Dickens's intimate friend, as did another contributor of that paper, William Johnson Fox.'

Page 239: 'After the death of Mr Lynn in 1855 the property (Gads Hill) was in the market. Dickens, who was intimate with Miss Lynn, to whom as we have seen…'

And from Una Pope-Hennessy's biography of Dickens[43] we have in Chapter 24, Page 426: 'To those who knew him intimately his life appeared to have changed in quality. The old equal friendships were a thing of the past, they had been replaced by intimacies with younger men, like Wilkie Collins, George Sala, Percy Fitzgerald, Edmund Yates.'

So, unless one wishes to make a case that as well as with Ellen Ternan, Dickens also had sexual relationships with several women, and an even greater number of men, one should be very careful in the interpretation of the word 'intimacy' as used, perhaps, by Ellen, relayed by Benham, and eventually reported by Thomas Wright.

As I said, all very interesting, but telling us nothing about the real nature of the relationship between Charles Dickens and Ellen Ternan.

The final piece that also falls into this group is a letter Dickens wrote to his friend Mrs Frances Elliot.[44] Of course we do not have the letter from Mrs Elliot that prompted Dickens to write, but clearly it seems she had been asking some probing questions about Ellen, and had perhaps expressed a wish to meet her. Mrs Elliot was known to Tom Trollope and his wife, who as we have seen was Ellen's eldest sister, and it is possible that Mrs Elliot had heard something from them that had raised her curiosity. Without the original letter Dickens's responses are somewhat unclear, although very protective of Ellen. In this letter Dickens strongly expressed the view that it would be inexpressibly painful to Ellen to think that Mrs Elliot knew her history and he believed that it would distress her for the rest of her life. He feared that meeting Mrs Elliot would destroy her self-reliance which had got her through so much.

Other parts of Dickens's letter give the impression that he may have fallen out with Mrs Trollope over something that was not made clear, but there is no later evidence of a falling out with Tom himself. It is Dickens's use of the words 'know her history' that I think deserves a comment. 'History' carries connotations of something in the past, rather than the present, that Ellen might find upsetting. Had the references been about the possibility of Ellen being Dickens's mistress, i.e., in the present, the word 'situation' would have been more appropriate. Rather, I think Dickens used the word 'history' deliberately, referring to some facts from her past, her illegitimacy perhaps, that she has, of necessity, borne alone, and she would not want that to be known by Mrs Elliot, or indeed anybody else. But like the other examples referred to earlier, this really gives us very little, apart from another opportunity for speculation.

While we are looking at Ellen's sister, Frances Trollope née Ternan, it is worth noting how easy it is for two half-truths to be combined into a monstrous non-truth. This, from the internet:

Ternan, Frances Eleanor (c. 1803–1873)

English actress and writer. Name variations: Frances Eleanor Trollope; Frances Eleanor Jarman; Mrs. Ternan. Born Frances Eleanor Jarman around 1803; died in 1873; second wife of Thomas Adolphus Trollope (1810–1892, a novelist); daughter-in-law of *Frances Milton Trollope* (1779–1863).

Frances Eleanor Ternan made her first stage appearance at Bath, England, in 1815. At Covent Garden in 1827–28, she appeared as Juliet to Charles Kemble's

Romeo. Ternan accompanied her first husband on an American and Canadian tour in 1834–36. She appeared as Pauline in *The Winter's Tale* (1855) and as blind Alice in *The Bride of Lammermoor* (1866). Following her second marriage to Thomas Adolphus Trollope, Ternan left the stage, settled in Florence, and wrote *Aunt Margaret's Trouble* (1866), *Black Spirits and White* (1877), and *That Unfortunate Marriage* (1888). With her husband, she also published *Homes and Haunts of the Italian Poets* (1881).

Quite clearly the unnamed author of this piece has taken the first part of *Mrs* Frances Eleanor Ternan's life, and merged it into the second part of *Miss* Frances Eleanor Ternan's life to create two half-truths squashed into a complete falsehood. The website containing this item, Ternan, Frances Eleanor (c. 1803–1873) | Encyclopedia.com has had in excess of three million views, so there are now probably more than a few people who believe that Ellen's mother, rather than her sister, became Tom Trollope's second wife!

Epilogue and Post Script

Because it is so unbelievable, the truth often escapes being known.

Heraclitus

In the foregoing chapters of this little volume I have not tried to disprove the common belief that Ellen was Dickens's mistress and gave birth to his child. Rather, I have tried to provide a reasoned alternative to challenge that commonly held belief. There are three possible relationships: platonic, carnal or filial. Given the generosity Dickens showed toward the Ternan family, and his secretiveness, I think one could rule out the platonic option. As a scientist, I found I could not accept the complaisance with which most commentators on Charles Dickens have accepted as fact the Wright/Storey narrative, based as it is on such a woeful lack of irrefutable evidence without questioning that view. I have no additional evidence beyond that put forward by everyone else, except that I have included words written by Dickens himself in his fictions and in his letters, prior to 1858 when the whole debacle 'kicked off'. In weighing the evidence originating after 1857/8, I find it can all go on *both* the 'Mistress' and the 'Daughter' pans of the balance with equal weight, thereby not providing much help. However, that originating prior to 1857 can *only* be placed on the 'Daughter' pan, and clearly swings the balance towards that conclusion. Thus, rather than embarking on this study with a pre-formed opinion, I have let the conclusion that the relationship was filial rather than carnal develop out of the review of all the available information.

So, to summarise the whole saga:

Yes, Dickens did have an affair with an actress, as stated by Thackeray.

Yes, that actress did carry his child, as stated by Storey.

No, the child was not a boy who died; but a girl, Ellen, who survived.

No, the actress was not Ellen Ternan, but her mother, Frances Ternan.

On the balance of probabilities, I believe that Ellen was most likely the innocent victim of circumstances beyond her control, and was not the greedy little gold-digging mistress she was often portrayed to be in the many tarnished portraits that have been published since 1935. I hope that this volume, presenting an untarnished portrait of Ellen, will at least encourage future students, scholars and commentators to keep a more open mind as they write and talk about her.

Acknowledgements

Writing in antipodean isolation, physically far away from London and the hub of the Dickensian world, it becomes necessary to rely on the works of those who, over many years, have provided enormous amounts of information and some great insights into the life of Charles Dickens. In roughly chronological order, I will mention the biographies by John Forster, Peter Ackroyd, Michael Slater, Clare Tomalin, Lillian Nayder and Helena Kelly as being the books on which I have placed most reliance for general background information. Of these authors, I had the pleasure of meeting Michael Slater in 2012 at the Dickens Fellowship Conference in Portsmouth, on which occasion he generously found time to read an early manuscript of a paper I was working on at that time, and it was his encouragement that persuaded me to continue delving further into Dickens's life. I have also been fortunate enough to have met with Lillian Nayder when she visited Australia a few years ago, and to have had some email correspondence with Helena Kelly. I regret that I have not had an opportunity to meet or communicate with Peter Ackroyd or Claire Tomalin, but I sincerely admire their research and have found their work to be invaluable.

Since embarking on this project, many people have helped and contributed in many different ways. In chronological order, to the dedicatee of this book, Dr Alan Dilnot, I owe so much for his help, advice and encouragement from the time we first met right up to the submission of the manuscript. Also, many thanks to a very good friend, Dr Brian Chapman, early enthusiastic discussions with whom spurred me on my way. Dr Emily Bell, the immediate past Editor of *The Dickensian,* provided much guidance and encouragement in the development of the paper in which I first suggested that the relationship between Dickens and Ellen was that of father and daughter. Next came my friend and neighbour Marjorie Wardlaw, friend and colleague Professor Stephen Cordner, and friend and member of the Melbourne Branch of the Charles Dickens Fellowship Barbara Sharpe, who generously gave of their time to read and provide invaluable commentary on the drafts of the book as they developed. I am also grateful to the staff of the Sir Louis Matheson Library at Monash University in general, and to the Rare Books Department in particular, for access to books I could not otherwise have read. Emma Harper of the Charles Dickens Museum provided electronic copies of photographs and of documents that I could not otherwise have seen, living as I do in Melbourne, so far from London.

When it came to publishing, Amy Jordan of Pen and Sword was able to set me on the right path, and then did a great job of steering me through the arcane intricacies of the publishing process. Karyn Burnham did a marvellous job of editing, and Jon Wilkinson produced a great cover design.

I am also grateful to have received, from a most unexpected quarter, help and guidance in the overall structure of the text. Whilst researching Ellen's brother-in-law Tom Trollope, I strayed into the life of his brother Anthony, and a book describing Anthony Trollope's visits to Australia authored by Dr Nigel Starck. I had a school chum with that name whom I had lost contact with in 1958, and to my amazement I discovered that this was indeed my chum Nigel! Having made a very successful career in journalism Nigel was an ideal person with whom I could discuss the actual structure of my book. So very many thanks to the brothers Trollope for bringing Nigel and myself back together!

To my family, Helen, Peej and Amy-Ann, and to my golfing mates, I say thank you for putting up with my banging on about Ellen, frequently at the most inappropriate times!

To all of these wonderful people, some of whom I have never met, I shall be forever grateful.

Appendix

Dramatis Personae

Very brief biographical details of everyone mentioned through the text, to enable the reader to see how and why they fit into the narrative.

Ackroyd, Peter b. 1949	British biographer and novelist, with a special interest in history and the culture of London. His biographies include Charles Dickens, and the poets William Blake and T.S. Elliot. He has also written a 'biography' of London. He is a Fellow of the Royal Society of Literature, and was appointed a Commander of the Order of the British Empire in 2003.
Anderson, Hans Christian (1805–1875)	Danish writer, best known for his fairy tales. He was well known to Dickens, and stayed with him at Gad's Hill, possibly outstaying his welcome!
Anderson, James Robertson (1811–1895)	Anderson was born in Scotland. His father was an actor, and James's first stage appearance was when he was a toddling 2-year-old. He continued with his acting career in the provinces, and eventually tried his hand at theatre management. He then moved to London and made his debut there in 1837 with Macready. He spent a year in

	America before returning to London. The Theatre Royal, Drury Lane was cleaned and refurbished in 1847, after which, in 1849, Anderson became the lessee. However, he retired in 1851 having accrued debts of the order of £5,000. He returned to full-time acting, even travelling to Australia, where he met with mixed success. On his return to England, he wrote his own plays, but in February 1895, on his way home from the Garrick Club, he was attacked and garrotted, injuries from which he failed to recover. He died on 3 March.
Austin, Alfred (1835–1913)	British poet, appointed Poet Laureate in 1896 succeeding Tennyson. His work had received mixed reviews, with some saying he was an unworthy choice. He was a friend of Thomas Adolphus Trollope, whose second wife was Frances Eleanor Ternan, Ellen's eldest sister.
Bazelgette, Sir Joseph (1819–1891)	A civil engineer, he was put in charge of the reconstruction of the London sewage system following the Great Stink of the 1850s and the deadly outbreaks of cholera.
Beadnell, Maria (1810–1886)	Dickens's first adolescent love, the daughter of a senior banking clerk. Dickens met her in early 1830, and the relationship lasted about three years. Maria was pretty, well educated, but brought up expected to do very little for herself. She had a tendency to tease, and was a little flirtatious. Their relationship ended in May 1833. Maria went on to marry Mr Henry Winter. Dickens met again with the widowed Mrs Winter in 1854.

Bechhofer Roberts, Carl Eric (1894–1949)	A British writer also qualified in law, he was private secretary to Lord Birkenhead for a time. He wrote non-fiction on a number of subjects including biography, travel and politics under his own name, and he also wrote about fifteen fictions, some, including *This Side Idolatory,* under the pen-name Ephesian.
Benham, Rev. William (1831–1910)	Ordained deacon in 1857 and priest in 1858, Benham was highly thought of and was eventually made one of the 'Six Preachers' of Canterbury. He was given the vicarage of Margate in 1872 where, among other matters, he became the chairman of the first school board in 1880. He certainly would have met and known Ellen as the wife of the head of one of the town schools. A keen fan of Charles Dickens, he served as a vice-president of the Fellowship for a while. He was also a literary scholar of note, editing an edition of the poetry of William Cowper. It is probably through that interest that he was known to Thomas Wright of Olney who was also very much involved in preserving the works of Cowper.
Bowen, John	Professor of nineteenth-century Literature at the University of York. His main areas of research are nineteenth- and twentieth-century fiction, but he has also written on modern poetry and essays on literary theory. He is a member of the Advisory Board of the Clarendon Edition of the works of Dickens, and has written or edited many books, academic articles and chapters. He has served as President of the Dickens Fellowship.

Bradford, Gamaliel (1866–1932)	Despite suffering poor health during most of his life, Bradford wrote 114 biographies over a period of twenty years, and is regarded as the American pioneer of the psychographic form of written biographies, following the style developed by Lytton Strachey. As well as his output of biographies, he was a poet, dramatist and critic.
Brown, Rosalind	Not a lot is known. Rosalind was a widow whom Ellen met in Italy following the death of Dickens. They became friends, and Ellen lodged with Rosalind as a paying guest on her return to England. Rosalind was instrumental in nursing Ellen back to health from whatever it was that ailed her in 1873. They remained good friends, as did Ellen's daughter Gladys and Rosalind's daughter Helen, who were brought up together.
Browne, Hablot Knight (Phiz) (1815–1882)	Phiz was born in England, as the fourteenth child of Catherine and William Loder Browne's fifteen children. However, according to his biographer Valerie Browne Lester (his great-great-granddaughter), he was actually the illegitimate son of his putative eldest sister Kate, and a Captain Nicholas Hablot. After a disrupted childhood (William Browne abandoned the family and fled to America) he was apprenticed to an engraver, and later became the preferred illustrator of Dickens's novels, while also in demand by other authors.

Buckstone, John Baldwin (1802–1879)	An English playwright and actor particularly noted for comedy. Having studied law and being articled to a solicitor, he abandoned that in favour of acting, finding a mentor in Edmund Kean. As well as starring in his own plays, of which he wrote over 150, he was also manager of the Haymarket Theatre from 1853 to 1877. However, despite his undoubted popularity and acting skills, he made some bad investments and eventually ill health and bankruptcy forced him to retire in 1877. Dying in 1879 it has been claimed that his ghost has often been seen at the Haymarket Theatre, particularly during comedies.
Burdett-Coutts, Angela (1814–1906)	First Baroness Burdett-Coutts, the daughter of Sir Francis Burdett and his wife Sophia, née Coutts. On the death of her grandfather, she inherited his estate (approx. £200 million today) and became one of the richest women in England. Her association with Dickens was purely philanthropic, when she became the generous supporter of Urania Cottage, a home for homeless women – more commonly referred to now as a home for fallen women. Their friendship cooled after Dickens and Catherine separated.
Callow, Simon (b. 1949)	A very successful British actor, director and writer, his first great acting success being the title role in the play *Amadeus* in 1979. He went on to receive many awards for both stage and screen productions, and portrayed Dickens

	in many television productions. His biography of Dickens, published in 2012 (the 200th anniversary of the birth of Dickens) has the title *Charles Dickens and the Great Theatre of the World*.
Collins, Charles (1828–1873)	The younger brother of Wilkie Collins, Charley (as he was known) was associated with the Pre-Raphaelite Brotherhood, but while his membership was proposed by Millais, he was rejected by Rossetti. He fell in love with Rossetti's sister Maria, but she rejected him. In 1860 he married Dickens's younger daughter Katey, and was later engaged to illustrate *The Mystery of Edwin Drood*. However, his health deteriorated and he was unable to do more than the cover illustration. He died from cancer in 1873.
Collins, Wilkie (1824–1889)	A novelist and playwright, he is best known for *The Woman in White* and *The Moonstone*. He is considered to be the 'father' of crime fiction and detective novels. He met Dickens in 1850 and they became firm friends, often travelling together and collaborating. Some of his work was published in *Household Words*. Wilkie lived an unconventional private life, openly maintaining two mistresses, one a widow with a daughter by her late husband, and the other, a younger woman with whom he had three children.

Copernicus, Nicolaus (1473–1543)	A mathematician, astronomer and Catholic canon, Copernicus formulated a model of the universe putting the sun at the centre, rather than the earth. His major work *On the Revolutions of the Celestial Spheres* was published just before he died. He was something of a polymath, becoming prominent in the fields of economics, medicine and politics in addition to his mathematics and astronomy.
Dickens, John (1785–1851)	The father of Charles Dickens, John was the posthumous son of his father William Dickens, who was butler to the wealthy Crewe family. His mother was the housekeeper. Thus, he grew up in an environment where money was not a problem, and that might have contributed to his life-long tendency to spend more than he earned. Whatever the root cause of his profligacy, throughout his working life as a clerk in the naval pay office he was frequently in debt, eventually being incarcerated in the Marshalsea prison while the young Charles worked in some capacity for a blacking company.
Dickens, Charles Culliford Boz (1837–1896)	The first child born to Dickens and Catherine. When he was 10 he attended the junior department of Kings College, after which he went to Eton, the fees being paid by Angela Burdett-Coutts. While he showed promise as a journalist, his father thought he should go into business, and he started at

	Barings Bank. He started a printing business, but after that failed, he joined *All the Year Round* with his father. Charles married and had one son and seven daughters, who were left in fairly dire straits when he died, leaving an estate of something less than £20.
Dickens, Edward Bulwer Lytton (Plorn) (1852–1902)	The last child born to Dickens and Catherine, and always known as 'Plorn', he migrated to Australia following his brother Alfred. Initially working on a cattle station, he became manager of Mount Murchison Station at Wilcannia in New South Wales. He married Constance Dessailly, the daughter of a local property owner, and opened his own stock agency. However, he experienced severe losses, and borrowed from his brother Henry, still in the UK. He entered politics and was elected to the NSW Legislative Assembly in 1889, but was defeated the following election in 1894. He was then appointed as a rabbit inspector for the Moree district, and died there in 1902. He never repaid the debt to his brother.
Dickens, Elizabeth née Barrow (1789–1863)	The mother of Charles. By all accounts, Elizabeth was an intelligent woman, with a gift for storytelling. According to Peter Ackroyd, their relationship was complex, and established on guilt and rejection, combined with a kind of hopeless love. He was to say that he never could forgive, nor forget, that his mother was warm for him to continue at the blacking factory after the release of his father from the Marshalsea.

Dickens, Mary, (always known as Mamie, but I have decided to retain her given name of Mary) (1838–1896)	Nick-named 'Mild Glo'ster' by her father because of her personality, Mary was named for her mother's sister Mary, who had died in the previous year. Her Godfather was John Forster. Mary never married, and lived with the family till well after Dickens's death in 1870. She continued to live with her aunt Georgina, but that relationship cooled as Georgina had difficulty living with Mary who apparently 'drunk too much'. But Georgina and Mary jointly edited a small collection of Dickens's letters, published in 1880. She also wrote *The Charles Dickens Birthday Book*, with illustrations by her sister Katey, *Charles Dickens by his Eldest Daughter* (1885), and *My Father as I Recall Him* (1896), and a short story, *The Staircase at Fairlawn Manor* (1891). After Dickens's death, Mary left Gad's Hill and Georgina to live for many years out of London with a 'disreputable clergyman and his wife'.
Elliot, Mrs Frances	A friend of Dickens, also known to the Trollopes. A wealthy Scottish heiress, she divorced her first husband on the grounds of his adultery and violence after the case was taken all the way to the House of Lords. She remarried, but that was not very satisfactory. A writer of several novels, she was popular in her day, but now largely forgotten. She also wrote for *Bentley's Miscellany*, was friendly with Wilkie Collins, and through him, met Dickens.

Fechter, Charles (1824–1879)	Originally studying to be a sculptor, he later became a successful actor, eventually moving from the Continent to London where he met and befriended Dickens and Wilkie Collins. He later moved to America, and after mixed success, lived the last three years in seclusion on a small farm.
Forster, John (1812–1876)	An exact contemporary of Dickens, Forster studied law, but never practised. Instead he became a literary and dramatic critic and a successful biographer. As his reputation spread, he became friendly with many writers, including Dickens, with whom his friendship was lifelong. Forster became one of Dickens's closest confidants, reading all the novels in manuscript, and Dickens frequently took Forster's advice. Forster married in 1857 and the friendship seemed to cool a little in the 1860s, but was revived toward the end of Dickens's life. Maybe the cooling had more to do with Forster spending more time with his wife than with the men? Dickens bequeathed all of his manuscripts to Forster, who in turn bequeathed them to the South Kensington Museum.
Freud, Sigmund (1856–1939)	An Austrian neurologist and the founder of what became known as psychoanalysis. His theories provided a clinical method for evaluating and treating pathologies seen as originating from conflicts in the psyche.

Harraden, Beatrice (1864–1936)	Harraden was a British writer, her best-selling work being *Ships That Pass in the Night*. A staunch supporter of the women's suffrage movement, she was both a leader and a founding member of the Women's Social and Political Union and an integral part of the Women Writers' Suffrage League and the Women's Tax Resistance League.
Harrison, Michael (1907–1991)	Michael Harrison was the pen name of author Maurice Desmond Rohan, a Sherlock Holmes scholar better known for his detective fiction.
Hawksley, Lucinda (b. 1977)	A great-great-great-granddaughter of Dickens, Lucinda Hawksley is an author, travel writer and lecturer with a Master of Arts in literature and the history of art. Her impressive list of publications includes several on Charles Dickens in addition to *Katey; The Life and Loves of Dickens's Artist Daughter*.
Hogarth, Catherine (1815–1879) Wife of Dickens	Born in Scotland, Catherine was the eldest daughter of George Hogarth. Hogarth became a writer and music critic for the *Morning Chronical* at the time that Dickens was a young journalist there. Later, Hogarth became editor of the *Evening Chronical* and commissioned Dickens to write some sketches for the newspaper. It was through this link that Dickens met Catherine shortly after his romance with Maria Beadnell came to an end. Catherine and Dickens became engaged, and married soon after on the strength of the income he was receiving

	for *Pickwick Papers*. They went on to have ten children, and despite many early letters expressing happiness together, Dickens became increasingly distant from her, until they finally separated in 1858.
Hogarth, Georgina (1827–1917)	Sister of Catherine, sister-in-law of Dickens. Shortly after Catherine and Dickens married, Catherine's sister Mary came on an extended stay with them, a practice not uncommon at that time. However, Mary died very suddenly, and during her next pregnancy, the younger Georgina came to stay. That visit lasted until Dickens's death. Georgina became aunt, nursemaid and nanny to all the Dickens children, as well as companion to Catherine. She travelled wherever the Dickenses went, except on the trip to America, during which she looked after the children left at home. There were various claims and accusations of an affair between Dickens and Georgina, none of which appear to have any substance. Georgina and Ellen Ternan were on very friendly terms.
Hogarth, Mary (1819–1837)	Catherine's sister, who came to stay with the Dickenses following the birth of their first child Charley. Apparently more vivacious than Catherine, the relationship with Dickens himself appears to have been very close. However, she died shortly after returning home from the theatre, and many biographers

	have commented on the effect that her death might have had on Dickens. Scholars have noted the 'presence' of Mary in characters such as Rose Maylie (*Oliver Twist*), and Agnes Wickfield (*David Copperfield*).
Jerichau-Baumann, Elisabeth (1819–1881)	Born in Warsaw, her parents were of German extraction. She studied art in Dusseldorf, and began exhibiting there in 1844. She moved to Rome, but also had great success in France and London, where Queen Victoria requested a private showing at Buckingham Palace, on which occasion she presented the Queen with an 1850 portrait of Hans Christian Andersen. Baumann married Jens Adolf Jerichau, a professor of art in Rome, and they had nine children, two of whom died in infancy. Of those surviving, several became artists, and a grandson, J.A. Jerichau became one of Denmark's most talented modernist painters.
Jerrold, Douglas (1803–1857)	The son of an actor, Jerrold joined the navy when he was 10 years old, serving under Jane Austen's brother, Charles Austen. After two years he left the sea to become a compositor, and also started writing poetry with some success. He later started writing satirical plays, and earned the nickname 'Little Shakespeare in a camlet cloak'. His best known play *Black-Eyed Susan* was a great success, and cemented his reputation as a dramatist. In 1851 he acted with Dickens in a production of the Bulwer Lytton play *Not So Bad As We Seem*.

	As well as being a dramatist, Jerrold was also a successful journalist, contributing to *Punch* among other periodicals. One article in *Punch* about the forthcoming great exhibition of 1851 included the phrase 'the Palace of very crystal', giving rise to the name by which the Crystal Palace has been known ever since.
Kean, Charles (1811–1868)	The son of actor Edmund Kean, Charles was an Irish-born English actor and theatre manager eventually specialising in Shakespeare. Initially not achieving much success in London, Kean moved to Glasgow where he acted with his father to greater acclaim. He toured in the USA with much success, and later returned to London playing Hamlet, which established his place among the top tragedians of the time.
Kelly, Helena (b.1981)	Helena Kelly was raised in the North Kent Marsh area, so well-known to Dickens. She holds a doctorate from the University of Oxford, where she has taught Classics and English literature. As well as her biography of Dickens, she has previously published a biography of Jane Austen. She is currently a Visiting Scholar at the Oxford Centre for Life-Writing.
Landor, Walter Savage (1775–1864)	Landor was an English writer, poet and activist. While highly respected as a poet and writer by his contemporary poets and critics, he did not achieve much popular acclaim during his lifetime. However, he was appreciated by younger writers, and certainly influenced several of the next generation, including Dickens.

Longley, Katharine (1920–2009)	Graduated with a BA Honours degree in Classics from University College London in 1941. She worked as a librarian prior to undertaking an Archive Diploma Course, and then became a part-time archivist for York Minster Library. Later she became friendly with Helen Wickham, the daughter of Mrs Rosalind Brown. Helen had been very friendly with Ellen's daughter Gladys, and accordingly was able to give Katherine Longley a good insight into Ellen's life.
Lynn Linton, Elizabeth (1822–1898)	The youngest of twelve children, her father was a vicar, the Rev. James Lynn. She left home in 1845 and moved to London where her career as a writer was fostered by William Ainsworth and Walter Savage Landor. However, neither of her first two novels met with any great success, and she turned to journalism, joining the staff of the *Morning Chronicle* becoming the first female journalist to receive a salary. She became a regular contributor to several periodicals, including Dickens's *All the Year Round*. Through this connection, she became very friendly with Harry Wills, Dickens's sub-editor. In 1858 Eliza, as she was generally known, married a Mr Linton, an eminent wood engraver and poet, and moved to his house in the Lake District, together with his seven children by his previous wife. They separated on friendly terms in 1867, he going to America,

	and she returning to London to pursue her career as a writer. It was at this stage that she started meeting with success as a novelist. Despite her career demonstrating her strength as a woman in a previously male-dominated world, including her being elected to the Society of Writers and being the first woman to serve on its committee, many of her essays had a decidedly strong anti-feminist bent. She claimed not to have known Dickens very well, despite Thomas Wright claiming that Dickens and she were 'intimate'. On the death of her father, she inherited Gad's Hill Place, which she subsequently sold to Dickens.
Maclise, Daniel, (1806–1870)	Maclise RA was an Irish-born artist and illustrator, most of his working life spent in England. His first brush with fame came when he took an opportunity to make a surreptitious sketch of Sir Walter Scott, which he later lithographed. The popularity of the prints led to many commissions for portraits. A later lithograph of the actor Charles Kean also secured Maclise a considerable income. He not only painted a portrait of Dickens, they became very friendly, and Maclise illustrated several of Dickens's Christmas books and other works.

Macready, William (1793–1873)	The son of the Irish actor William Macready the Elder, he was born in London, and educated at Rugby School. He had intended going on to university, but his father's financial difficulties led to him joining his father in the theatre. His first appearance was as Romeo in 1810, which met with critical acclaim. He shortly after fell out with his father and went off on his own to Bath and other provincial centres. Initially concentrating on romantic drama, he met with great success as a tragedian. But in addition to Shakespeare and the classic repertoire, Macready was also very willing to support contemporary English drama. Macready had acted Hamlet to Frances Ternan's (Ellen's mother) Ophelia, and while he was not fond of Mr Ternan, remained very friendly and supportive of Mrs Ternan. Introduced to Dickens by Forster just as Dickens was making his name as an author, his friendship with Dickens lasted until Dickens's death.
Nayder, Lillian (b.1957)	Lillian Nayder is Professor of English at Bates College, Lewiston, Maine, specialising in nineteenth-century British fiction, including Jane Austen, the Brontës, Dickens, Wilkie Collins and Victorian crime fiction.

Nicoll, Sir William Robertson (1851–1923)	The son of a Free Church minister, he was ordained in 1874, but retired in 1885 following an attack of typhoid which severely damaged his lung. He was a man of letters, and became the editor of *The Expositor* for Hodder and Stoughton, remaining in that position until his death. In that position, he recruited many exceptional writers for the paper, including J.M. Barrie, and, presumably, Mrs Lynn Linton.
Nisbet, Ada (1907–1994)	Professor Emerita of UCLA, Nisbet was a highly regarded Dickensian scholar and was firmly wedded to the Wright/Storey narrative about Ellen.
Ockham's Razor	Also spelled Occam's or Ocham's Razor. Attributed to the fourteenth-century philosopher William of Ockham, it is the principle that recommends solving problems by seeking explanations requiring the smallest number of elements. Put in more everyday English, the simplest explanation is usually the best one.
Olliffe, Sir Joseph (1808–1869)	Born in Ireland, he was educated in Paris, graduating as Doctor of Medicine in 1840. In 1846 he was appointed a Knight of the Legion of Honour by Louis Phillipe; in 1852 he was appointed as physician to the British Embassy in Paris, and knighted at Buckingham Palace a year later. He was promoted to the rank of Officer by Napoleon III in 1855. He had a large private practice, and a considerable social standing.

Ouvry, Frederic (1814–1881)	Lawyer and antiquarian. He was a friend of, and the solicitor for, Dickens.
Perugini, Katey née Dickens (1839–1929)	Full name Catherine Elisabeth Macready Dickens, but generally known as Katey, she appeared to have been a lively child, who earned the nickname 'Lucifer Box' because of her quick temper. She was quick to learn, and was proficient in French and Italian. Her first marriage to Charles Collins (Wilkie's brother) was marred by his chronic illness, and on his death, she married the artist Carlo Perugini. Katey herself was a very competent artist, mostly painting children on commission. Unfortunately, it appears that very few of her works are available in the public domain. The Peruginis had one child, a son who died in infancy. In her later years she befriended Gladys Storey, and out of that friendship came the book *Dickens and Daughter*. Her life is well told in Lucinda Hawksley's biography *Katey, The Life and Loves of Dickens's Artist Daughter*.
Pope-Hennessy, Una DBE (1875–1949)	Dame Una Pope-Hennessy was a British writer, historian, and biographer. The daughter of Sir Arthur Birch, she married Major (later Major-General) Richard Pope-Hennessy in 1910. She was appointed Dame Commander of the Order of the British Empire (DBE) in 1920 for her work on the Committee for Prisoners of War. In addition to her biography of Dickens, she also wrote on Frances Trollope, Fanny Kemble and Harriet Martineau as well as Edgar Allan Poe.

Dramatis Personae 169

Robinson, George Wharton (1851–1910)	The husband of Ellen. Ordained as a deacon, but following his marriage to Ellen, gave up the pastoral life to run a school for boys in Margate, Kent. However, for reasons that are not particularly clear, his health deteriorated, and they had to give up the school and leave Margate. After trying to run a market garden, with no great success, in 1907 Ellen was operated on for breast cancer, and despite her age, made a good recovery. However it took its toll on Wharton, who, never strong, fell ill himself, and died three years later.
Rogers, Samuel (1763–1855)	British poet. The son of a banker, he also went into banking and became a very wealthy man. He was also a highly successful poet and art collector who developed a reputation for hosting elaborate breakfast parties to which the literati of the day were invited.
Sainte-Beuve, Charles Augustin (1804–1869)	Born in Boulogne, he studied medicine before developing a career in literary and artistic criticism. A friendship that developed between Sainte-Beuve and Victor Hugo following his writing favourable reviews of Hugo's work, cooled when Sainte-Beuve had an affair with Hugo's wife.
Sedgwick, Amy. Née Sarah Gardiner. (1835–1897)	Was a celebrated actor, developing her craft in the provinces prior to moving to London in 1857. An accomplished Shakespearean actor, she was also commended for her portrayal of Dickens's character Sergeant Buzfuz in a charity concert in 1871.

Shakespeare, William (1564–1616)	English playwright and poet.
Slater, Michael MBE	Professor Emeritus of Birkbeck, University of London, is one of the most highly regarded Dickens scholars, for his research, his publications, and for his generosity as a teacher.
Smith, George (1824–1901)	Smith's father in partnership with Alexander Elder started the publishing house of Smith and Elder. George junior inherited the business on his father's death, and went on to become extremely successful, publishing work for Ruskin, the Brontës, Darwin, Thackeray and Wilkie Collins among others.
Storey, Gladys (1897–1964)	The daughter of artist Graham Storey, began as an actress, but abandoned that career to become a writer. She had been introduced to Katey Perugini by her father in 1910, and in Katey's later years the Storeys, mother and daughter, 'monopolised' Katey to the chagrin of family members – 'one or other of the ubiquitous Storeys was always visiting'.
Strachey, Lytton (1880–1932)	An English writer and critic, he was a founding member of what became known as the Bloomsbury Set, a group of English intellectuals, writers and philosophers. As the author of *Eminent Victorians*, he established a new form of biography in which psychological insight and sympathy are combined with irreverence and wit, later known as psychographies or psychobiographies.

Taylor, William Rowland	The husband of Maria Ternan, Taylor was the son of a successful Oxford brewer. They married in June, 1863 and separated in 1873.
Ternan, Frances Eleanor, née Jarman, (1802–1873)	Born in Hull, Jarman was a daughter of actress Martha Mottershed. Her father had studied law, but worked as a theatre prompter when he married. Frances Jarman made her debut on stage with her mother prior to her christening, and continued acting in juvenile roles throughout her childhood. In 1834 she married Irish actor Thomas Ternan, and, following a successful trip to America (from which they returned with two daughters), they found work at the Theatre Royal Drury Lane. In 1839 she gave birth to a third daughter, Ellen. Mr Ternan died in 1846, and the Ternan ladies continued acting until 1857–8.
Thackeray, Anne (Lady Ritchie) (1837–1919)	The eldest daughter of William Thackeray, she and her younger sister were great friends of Dickens's daughters Mary and Katey. She was a successful writer, publishing several popular novels and short stories. She married her cousin Richmond Ritchie in 1877, becoming Lady Ritchie. She was also a step-aunt of Virginia Woolf.

Thackeray, William Makepeace (1811–1863)	Born in Calcutta, he was sent to England following the death of his father in 1815. He attended Trinity College Cambridge for a while, before travelling through Europe and squandering much of his inheritance on gambling and bad investments. He turned to journalism as a means of financial support, but his fame came with the publication of *Vanity Fair*. His earlier works were frequently savage attacks on 'society', military prowess, hypocrisy and marriage, usually under a variety of pseudonyms.
Thompson, (T.J.) Thomas James. (1811–1881)	T.J., the grandson and heir of Thomas Pepper Thompson, was the illegitimate son of James Thompson and his creole mistress Mary Edwards. T.J.'s first wife, Matilda, died in childbirth, and having been introduced to Christiana Weller by Dickens, he married her and had two more daughters. He was the brother-in-law of Dickens's solicitor, Charles Smithson, Partner of Mitton.
Tomalin, Claire (b. 1933)	An English biographer and journalist best known for her biographies of Thomas Hardy, Samuel Pepys, Jane Austen and Charles Dickens. Her book *The Invisible Woman, The Story of Nelly Ternan and Charles Dickens* was a best seller, and was made into a popular film. It is thanks to Claire Tomalin that we have so much detail about the lives of the Ternan family.

Trollope, Thomas Adolphus (Tom) (1810–1892)	An English author of over sixty books, but who spent most of his life in Italy. His first wife, Theodosia, with whom he had one daughter (Beatrice, generally known as Bice), was also a poet and writer. She died in 1865, after which Tom married Ellen's eldest sister Frances, who had been engaged by Tom to be Bice's governess.
Wagenknecht, Edward Charles. (1900–2004)	An American literary teacher, critic and author, his doctoral thesis was *The Man Charles Dickens: A Victorian Portrait*. As a critic, he was once described as 'one of the many book reviewers who ought to lose his job for not perceiving the merits and importance of William Gaddis's first novel, *The Recognitions*.' Also, he was roundly criticised by Ada Nisbet for daring to contradict those scholars who had accepted the Wright/Storey narrative about Ellen. In his memoir *As Far as Yesterday* (1968) he wrote 'I have always been more successful with book publishers than with magazine editors. Here, again, I am sure my irrefragable independence has been the root cause. Magazine editors have 'policies' and 'interests.' So have I, and I have never considered dropping mine to take up those of somebody else.'
Weller, Christiana (1825–1910)	Christiana was a very accomplished pianist whom Dickens saw performing at the age of 19. Some of his letters from that time seem to indicate an infatuation with her, and biographers have drawn a parallel with Mary Hogarth in Dickens's mind. She married T.J. Thompson, and had two children.

Wigan, Alfred Sydney (1814–1878)	An English actor and theatre manager, it is believed that he started his career as a singer, but by 1834 he was acting under the name Sydney Wigan at the Lyceum Theatre. Later he was at the newly built St James's Theatre, creating the role of John Johnson in Dickens's play *The Strange Gentleman*. A successful actor (he appeared in the first Royal Command Performance in 1848 by order of Queen Victoria) he was the actor–manager of the Olympic Theatre from 1853 to 1857, a position from which he retired due to ill health. However, two years later he returned to acting and theatre management, finally retiring in 1874.
Wills, William Henry (Harry) (1810–1880)	Known mostly for his close attachment to Dickens as sub-editor of *Household Words*, Wills was also a journalist and playwright. His father, a once wealthy ship owner, fell on hard times, and Wills, as he was generally referred to, was required to be the breadwinner for the family when his father died. Starting as a wood engraver, he took to journalism, eventually becoming sub-editor of *The Monthly Magazine*. After a varied contribution to journalism, he met Dickens in 1846 while the latter was editor of *The Daily News*, and shortly thereafter, joined Dickens as sub-editor of *Household Words* and of *All the Year Round*. Wills was a fluent writer, but somewhat pedantic, which amused Dickens. He later also took the job of secretary to Angela Burdett-Coutts, but a riding accident in 1868 left him with injuries from which he never really recovered.

Wilson, Sir Angus Frank (1912–1991)	During the Second World War, Wilson worked as a decoder at Bletchley Park. He then became superintendent of the Reading Room at the British Museum, a post which he eventually left in order to become a successful full-time writer, mostly of novels. Always interested in the life and works of Dickens, he published, in 1970, *The World of Charles Dickens*. He was knighted in 1980 for services to literature.
Wilson, Edmund (1895–1972)	An American biographer who was very interested in Dickens's personal life, and a follower of the psychographic school of thinking. He believed that Dickens's later novels were very much influenced by Ellen. He was very highly regarded by such Dickensian scholars as Ada Nisbet.
Wright, Thomas (1859–1936)	Wright was born, raised and lived his entire life at Olney. He was an antiquarian, with a great love of English poetry, especially that of William Cowper. He established, and became the head teacher of, the Cowper School at Olney, and was instrumental in the establishment of the Cowper Museum in that town. He was also a fan of Dickens, and takes some credit for suggesting the establishment of a Dickens Museum in London. His books included a *Life of Cowper*, several volumes of his own poetry, a *Life of Dickens* and his autobiography, published posthumously.

References

1. Wilson, A. *The World of Charles Dickens* (1972) Penguin Edition p.276
2. Harrison, M. *Charles Dickens: A Sentimental Journey in Search of an Unvarnished Portrait*, 1976
3. Wright, T., *The Life of Charles Dickens* 1935
4. Storey, G., *Dickens and Daughter* (1939) Frederick Muller Ltd London (1971 Haskell House)
5. Forster J. *The Life of Charles Dickens* (1872) London
6. *Thomas Wright of Olney: An Autobiography*, 1936
7. Maria Beadnell, 18 March 1833 *Pilgrim* Vol 1, p.16
8. Maria Beadnell, 14 May 1833 *Pilgrim* Vol 1, p.22
9. Maria Beadnell, 16 May 1833 *Pilgrim* Vol 1, p.72
10. Forster's *Life of Dickens* 1873
11. Catherine Hogarth, late May 1835 *Pilgrim* Vol 1, p.24
12. Bernard Darwin, *Dickens*, (1933) Duckworth, London
13. Nayder, Lillian, *The Other Dickens, a Life of Catherine Hogarth* (2011) Cornell University Press
14. Maclise, 16 August 1841, 'The Letters of Charles Dickens', *Pilgrim* Edition 7: (addendum) p.831
15. Tomalin, Claire, *Charles Dickens: A Life*, (2011) Viking, p.124
16. John Overs, 27 October, 1840, *Pilgrim* letters, 2:139-141
17. Wilkie Collins, 16 August 1859, *Pilgrim*, Vol 9; p.106
18. Nisbet, Ada, *Dickens and Ellen Ternan* (1952) University of California Press

19. Wilson, A. (1970) *The World of Charles Dickens* Penguin Edition 1972 p.276
20. Ackroyd, P. (1990) *Dickens*, Sinclair-Stevenson Ltd. p.913 et seq
21. Bowen, J. (2000), Bebelle and 'His Boots': Dickens, Ellen Ternan and the Christmas Stories.' *The Dickensian* 96 Part 3: pp.197–208
22. Wilkie Collins, 26 September 1854. *Pilgrim* Vol 7 p.423
23. Mrs A Brown, 24 October 1862. *Pilgrim* Vol 10, p.149
24. Ruck, B. (2014) 'Ellen Ternan and Charles Dickens: A Re-evaluation of the "Evidence".' *The Dickensian* 493.110.2 (2014): pp.118–130
25. Wills, *Pilgrim* Vol 10, p.146
26. Macready, 13 March 1838. *Pilgrim* Vol 1; p.386
27. Ackroyd, P. *Dickens* (1990) Sinclair-Stevenson Ltd. p.828
28. Slater, M. *The Great Charles Dickens Scandal*, (2012) Yale University Press p.11
29. Wills, *Pilgrim* Vol 8 p.448
30. Wills, *Pilgrim* Vol 8 p.451
31. Tomalin, Claire. 2011. *Charles Dickens: A Life* Viking, p.148
32. Wagenknecht, E. *Dickens and the Scandalmongers: Essays in Criticism* (1950)
33. Nisbet, A. (1952) *Dickens and Ellen Ternan*
34. The fourteenth-century English theologian and logician friar William of Ockham established the principle that 'entities must not be multiplied beyond necessity'. An interpretation of this principle, now known as Ockham's (or Occam's) Razor is that, of two theories, in the absence of definite proof of either, the one dependent on the fewest assumptions is more likely to be the correct one.
35. Callow, S. *Charles Dickens and the Great Theatre of the World* (2012) Harper Press

36. Longley, K. 'The Real Ellen Ternan' *The Dickensian* Vol 81 (1985)
37. Henry W. and Albert A. Berg Collection of English and American Literature, The New York Public Library. '[Diary, 1867. Holograph. Kept on the blank leaves of John Goldsmith's An almanack for the year of Our Lord 1867]' *The New York Public Library Digital Collections*. 1867. https://digitalcollections.nypl.org/items/c7609aa0-d473-013a-beba-0242ac110003
38. Curry, G. *Charles Dickens and Annie Fields* (1988) (Huntington Library)
39. Slater, M. *The Great Charles Dickens Scandal* (2012) Yale University Press p.94
40. Slater, M. *The Great Charles Dickens Scandal* (2012) Yale University Press p.181
41. Hawksley, L. *Katey The Life and Loves of Dickens's Artist Daughter* (2006) Random House
42. Lyn-Linton, E. *My Literary Life* (1899) Hodder and Stoughton, London
43. Pope-Hennessy, Una. *Charles Dickens* (1945) The Reprint Society
44. Letter to Frances Elliot (5 July 1867). *The Selected Letters of Charles Dickens* edited by Jenny Hartley Oxford University Press, p.410

Index

Ackroyd, Peter, 1, 21–2, 26, 29, 33–4, 79, 93, 95, 106–108, 129
Anderson, Hans Christian, 131
Anderson, James Robertson, 45
Austin, Alfred, 88

Bazelgette, Sir Joseph, 102
Beadnell, Maria, 4–5, 7, 41, 54, 57, 81, 91, 117
Bechhofer Roberts, Carl Eric, 54
Benham, Rev. William, 89–90, 126, 140–1
Bowen, John, 22–3, 25, 27
Bradford, Gamaliel, 10
Brown, Rosalind, 86, 88–90, 98
Browne, Hablot Knight (Phiz), 12
Buckstone, John Baldwin, 37–8, 56
Burdett-Coutts, Angela, 16

Callow, Simon, 96
Clennam, Arthur, 25, 38–40
Collins, Charles, 70
Collins, Wilkie, 15, 17, 24, 57, 70, 73, 77, 128, 141

Dickens, John, 2, 7, 29
Dickens, Catherine (née Hogarth), 7–9, 11–12, 14–16, 20, 26–9, 34, 41–2, 44–6, 48, 50, 54, 61–3, 66, 68–9, 72, 82, 115, 117–23, 125, 129–31, 133
Dickens, Charles Culliford Boz, 11, 14
Dickens, Edward Bulwer Lytton (Plorn), 14, 16
Dickens, Elizabeth (née Barrow), 2
Dickens, Mary, (aka Mamie), 12, 18, 20, 26, 28–9, 40, 42–3, 48–51, 70, 73, 85, 115, 122–3

Elliot, Frances, 141–2
Provis, Estella, 25, 80–1
Summerson, Esther, 25, 33, 35–8

Dombey, Florence, 33
Forster, John, 50, 90, 92, 123, 137–8, 140
Freud, Sigmund, 9–11, 21–2, 95

Harraden, Beatrice, 135
Harrison, Cora, 80, 82

Harrison, Michael, 71, 110
Hawksley, Lucinda, 120, 129–31, 139
Landless, Helena, 82
Hogarth, Catherine, *see* Dickens, Catherine
Hogarth, Georgina, 116, 123
Hogarth, Mary, 8–12, 21

Jerichau-Baumann, Elisabeth, 131
Jerrold, Douglas, 17, 52–3, 56, 134

Kean, Charles, 20
Kelly, Helena, 2

Landor, Walter Savage, 135, 137–8
Little Nell, 32
Longley, Katharine, 98, 108, 126–7
Lynn Linton, Elizabeth, 134–40

Maclise, Daniel, 15
Macready, William, 20, 26, 29, 32, 34, 49, 72, 97, 114
Manette, Lucie, 76, 78–9

Nayder, Lillian, 15
Nicoll, Sir William Robertson, 134
Nisbet, Ada, 19–21, 25, 94

Ockham's Razor, 96
Olliffe, Sir Joseph, 72–3
Ouvry, Frederic, 73

Perugini, Katey (née Dickens), 11, 52, 63, 70, 85, 103, 115–17, 124–5, 138
Pope-Hennessy, Una DBE, 95, 140
Robinson, George Wharton, 87–90, 118
Rogers, Samuel, 15

Sainte-Beuve, Charles Augustin, 9
Sedgwick, Amy (née Sarah Gardiner), 132
Shakespeare, William, 3, 19, 45, 128
Slater MBE, Michael, 1, 56, 63, 108, 120, 123, 127, 130–2
Smith, George, 88
Storey, Gladys, 11, 55, 103, 110, 115–16, 121, 123–5
Strachey, Lytton, 10

Taylor, Maria (née Ternan), 67–9, 72, 85, 87–8, 91–2
Taylor, William Rowland, 85
Ternan, Frances Eleanor (née Jarman), 20, 28, 67–9, 72, 87–8, 92, 113, 142–3
Thackeray, Anne (Lady Ritchie), 130, 138
Thackeray, William Makepeace, 61, 111, 136–7, 145

Thompson, Thomas James (T.J.), 10
Tomalin, Claire, 2, 58–9, 69, 90, 93, 97–8, 108, 113, 120, 128–9, 139
Trollope, Frances Eleanor (née Ternan), 142–3

Trollope, Thomas Adolphus (Tom), 68, 85, 141–3, 148
Twist, Oliver, 10, 13–14, 25–7, 29–30

Wagenknecht, Edward Charles, 94–5